JUNE 2022 EDITION

AN ANTHOLOGY OF ARTICLES

BRILLOPEDIA

Contents

Preface

"Start writing, no matter what. The water does not flow until the faucet is turned on".

-Louis L'Amour

This book is a bouquet of articles contributed by students, professors and academicians. Hundreds of students and professors are contributing their work to Brillopedia, we are here to provide ample information about Law and Contemporary issues. Our aim is to provide a platform for today's generation to express their views and ideas on law and contemporary law.

CHAPTER ONE

INTRODUCTION TO DEPOSITORY RECIEPTS

Author: Aryan Sinha, IV Year of B.B.A.,LL.B(Hons.) From Galgotias University.

Introduction

Depository Receipt is a negotiable certificate (negotiable instrument) issued by a bank in a domestic country that represents ownership of shares in companies of other countries. It is an important method of international funds among firms from emerging economies. Depository receipt is a form of indirect listing for international firms and they are allowed to cross list in other countries through the DR program.

In 1993, Central Government notified 'the Issue of Foreign Currency Convertible Bonds and Ordinary Shares (Through Depositary Receipt Mechanism) Scheme' to facilitate issuing of Foreign Currency Convertible Bonds and other Ordinary Shares in the foreign market through Depositary Receipt methods.

In 1996, depository got statutory recognition in India where "depository" means a company formed and registered under the Companies Act, 1956 & 2013 and its certificate of registration under "Section 12(1A) of the Securities and Exchange Board of India Act, 1992". The concept of 'depository' was included in "Indian company law 1996" through the Companies (Amendment) Act, 2000 and again reproduced in new "Indian company law 2013" also where 'depository' means a depository as defined Section 2(1)(e) of the Depositories Act, 1996. So depository must be a company as per company law and also must get registration certificate from SEBI.

In 2014, the Depository Receipts Scheme has been introduced by the Ministry of Finance on 21st October 2014 and came into force on 15th

December 2014. Subsequently the same has been also included by the Reserve Bank of India through the "Foreign Exchange Management (Transfer or issue of Security by a Person Resident outside India) (Seventeenth Amendment) Regulations, 2014."

As per "2014 Scheme - Depository Receipt" means a foreign currency denominated instrument, whether listed on an international exchange or not, issued by a foreign depository in a permissible jurisdiction on the back of eligible securities issued or transferred to that foreign depository and deposited with a domestic custodian and includes "'global depository receipt' as defined in section 2(44) of the Companies Act, 2013." Here, 'Foreign depository' means a person which has legal capacity to issue depository receipts in the permissible jurisdiction and this 'Permissible jurisdiction' means a foreign jurisdiction which is a member of the Financial Action Task Force on Money Laundering; and the regulator of the securities market in that jurisdiction is a member of the International Organization of Securities Commissions.

Schedule I of the Scheme has given a list of 34 countries as permissible jurisdiction including Argentina, United State, Australia, United Kingdom, Austria, Turkey, Belgium, Switzerland, Brazil, Sweden, Canada, Spain, China, South Africa, Denmark, Singapore, European Commission, Russian Federation, Finland, Portugal, France, Norway, Germany, New Zealand, Greece, The Netherlands, Mexico, Hong Kong, Luxembourg, Iceland, Republic of Korea, Ireland, Italy, Japan.

The shares of a company underlying the depository receipts shall form part of the public shareholding of the company under the Securities Contract (Regulation) Rules, 1957. If the holder of such depository receipts has the right to issue voting instruction then such depository receipts are listed on an international exchange.

Any Indian company (listed or unlisted, private or public) or any other issuer of permissible securities or any person holding permissible securities which has not been specifically prohibited from accessing the capital market or dealing in securities, are eligible to issue or transfer permissible securities to a foreign depository for the purpose of issue of depository receipts.

The domestic custodian shall ensure that the relevant provisions of the Scheme related to the issue and cancellation of depository receipts is complied with maintain records in respect of, and report to, Indian depositories all transactions in the nature of issue and cancellation of depository receipts for the purpose of monitoring limits under the "FEMA, 1999" and provide the information and data as may be called upon by SEBI, the RBI, Ministry of Finance, Ministry of Corporate Affairs and any other authority of law, and file with SEBI a copy of the document, by whether name called, which sets the terms of issue of depository receipts issued on the back of securities, as defined under "section 2(h) of the Securities Contracts (Regulation) Act, 1956 in a permissible jurisdiction".

Legislative Framework of Depository Receipts

1. Foreign Exchange Management (Transfer or issue of any foreign security) Regulations, 2000
2. The Companies (Global Depository Receipts) Rules, 2014
3. The Income Tax Act, 1961
4. Securities and Exchange Board of India (Issue of Capital and Disclosure Requirements) Regulations, 2009
5. The Foreign Currency Convertible Bonds and Ordinary Shares (Through Depository Receipts Mechanism) Scheme, 1993
6. Consolidated FDI Policy
7. The Depository Receipts Scheme, 2014

FDI Policy of Depository Receipts

Depository Receipts are traded on Stock Exchanges in the US, Singapore, Luxembourg, etc. Those are listed and traded in the US markets are known as American Depository Receipts (ADRs) and those listed and traded anywhere or elsewhere are known as Global Depository Receipts (GDRs).

"The proceeds of issues of Depository Receipts shall either be remitted to a bank account in India or deposited in an Indian bank operating abroad or any foreign bank (which is a Scheduled Bank under the "Reserve Bank of India Act, 1934") having operations in India with an agreement that the foreign bank having operations in India shall take responsibility for furnishing all the information which may be required and in the event of a sponsored issue of Depository Receipts, the proceeds of the sale shall be credited to the respective bank account of the shareholders."

"Domestic Custodian Bank means a banking company which acts as a custodian for the ordinary shares or foreign currency convertible bonds of an Indian company which are issued by it against global depository receipts or certificates."

"Overseas Depository Bank means a bank authorized by the issuing company to issue GDR against issue of Foreign Currency Convertible Bonds or ordinary shares of the issuing company."

Indian Depository Receipts

"Indian Depository Receipt means any instrument in the form of a depository receipt created by a domestic depository in India and authorized by a company incorporated outside India making an issue of such depository receipts".

- CHAPTER XA of the Securities and Exchange Board of India (Issue of Capital and Disclosure Requirements) Regulations, 2009 deals with 'Rights Issue of Indian Depository Receipts'.
- Chapter VII of the SEBI (Listing Obligations and Disclosure Requirements) Regulations, 2015 deals with 'Obligations of Listed Entity Which Has Listed Its Indian Depository Receipts'.
- The Security Exchange Board of India (Facilitation of Issuance of Indian Depository Receipts) (Amendment) Regulations, 2009.
- The Ministry of Corporate Affairs issued the Companies (Registration of Foreign Companies) Rules, 2014
- Indian Depository Receipts (IDRs) can be issued by nonresident companies in India subject to and under the terms and conditions of Companies (Issue of Depository Receipts) Rules, 2004 and subsequent amendment made thereto and the SEBI (ICDR) Regulations, 2000, as amended from time to time.

Indian legal framework for IDRs comprises

- Sections 2(48), 234, "390, and 469" of the Companies Act, 2013;
- Rule 13 of the Companies (Registration of Foreign Companies) Rules, 2014;
- Chapter X of the SEBI (Issue of Capital and Disclosure Requirements) Regulations, 2009;
- SEBI circulars dated August 28, 2012 and March 01, 2013.
- Schedule 7 of the FEMA 20;
- Part I, Section 4, Para 2 of the Master Circular on Foreign Investment in India;
- The Income Tax Act, 1961;

American Depository Receipts

American Depository Receipt (ADR) means a security issued by a bank or a depository in United States of America (USA) against underlying rupee shares of a company incorporated in India.

The ADRs are listed on the New York Stock Exchange (NYSE) and National Association Securities Dealers Automated Quotation (NASDAQ). ADR issues offer access to US institutional as well as retail markets while GDRs comprehensive disclosure and greater transparency as compared to GDR listing. GDRs can be converted to ADRs by surrendering the existing GDRs and depositing the underlying equity shares with ADR depository in exchange of ADRs. The issuing company has to comply with Security Exchange Commission (SEC) requirements to materialize the exchange offer process. However the company does not get any fund by this conversion of GDRs to ADRs.

CHAPTER TWO

ELUCIDATION AND EXPLICATION OF UNIFORM CIVIL CODE IN COROLLLARY WITH NUMEROUS FOLDS

Author: Ms.Shreya Lal, II Year of B.L.S.,LL.B from KLE College of Law, Navi Mumbai.

<u>Abstract</u>

India has always been the flag bearer of diversification and cultural manifolds. The settlement of foreign man in Indian soil and invasion of other realm inside the nation made it into a cradle of communities and religion. India as a nation till today stands rock solid in spite of variegated religions, communities, beliefs, nationalities, et cetera.

To govern and ensure smooth and sheen working of the nation and by its organs there are various bylaws also commonly known as personal laws made up for different branches of the Society.

Each fold has a different personal law to govern their people and let the good survive in harmony and the evil to pay off for their deeds. All of these laws of different columns lead to renunciation of human rights and humanity in colloquial sense.

The essence of a state resemblance to the great grandeur corollary to the uniform civil code landsus to the scripts of ancient and medieval history of the South Asian subcontinent aiming towards the ancient Vedic Hymns, to the Ashokan edicts also the great Mughal sovereign Akbar, can be said out loud as the predecessors of the Article 44 of the Indian constitution.

Returning to contemporary South Asia, the recent support for the codification of the reiteration seems problematic enough, and even more so in the given context, because in a situation very different from the circumstances that led the Constituent Assembly to use the questioned clause of DPSP, Article 44 reappeared the principle of national policy, even though there were subtle disputes on the floor of the assembly at that time. The paper here analyzes the historicalbackground of the unified civil encoding and formulates a provisional roadmap for such encodedtexts to adjust the optimal balance, so that a unified and complete melody represents the cultural diversity of India in the future.

Keywords: Uniform, civil, code, DPSP, Vedic, India.

<u>**Introduction**</u>

To start off with the abbreviation of Article 44 of the Indian constitution – UCC also commonly known as the uniform civil code in verbatim means the set of codification of laws of a subject with wide spectrum covered together and written to avoid dispute and draw a line between heterogeneity and homogeneity, also it mainly covers subject of personal laws (laws involved in person) or a group or class of people).

To state and codify the constitution here the article 44 which resides in the part IV of the book which is customarily termed as Directive Principles of State Policy.

'To step on the front foot of UCC, we may not proceed without a call out for religion.'

From the ages of history till today religion has gained global domination by various means of mythological edicts and also from various realm invasion and resettlement of Homo sapiens across the map.

Religion as taught and preached is about the supremacy of the almighty god, with effects from the ancient times in negligence of decades and centuries. As preached and exhibited the effects of religion can be found in personal laws so as they are created to differentiate between assorted classes and communities.

To renounce about every social and human gathering involving the community, we have personal laws for marriage, adoption, maintenance, inheritance, succession, separation, divorce, et cetera. Religion has resulted in enforcement and formation of personal laws to govern their legality and step forward in the paths of preaching the same.

Indian laws could be bifurcated into two vivid spectrums mainly- Personal law and Lex loci

(also known as law of the land or public law).

The former has a circumference of laws relating or involving an individual in regard to his/her duties, rights, responsibilities and correlation with the state, whereas the latter mentions about the laws that every person should abide to in concern tothe following territorial residence

Dr. B. R. Ambedkar sincerely said in the debates of the Constituent Assembly, "I personally do not understand why religion should be given this wide and wide-ranging jurisdiction to cover all life and prevent the invasion of this field."

Giving religion such a broad leeway in the judiciary that it cannot be questioned even in the event of a violation of human rights is not a good sign for any country, especially for a country like India, which promotes equality and justiceTherefore, the Uniform Civil Code, a common law for all indigenous peoples in the areas of marriage, divorce, adoption, alimony and inheritance , could be a permanent and wise solution toviolations of people's rights through the abuse of religious beliefs.

The talks and inevitability of Uniform codification resides in the scriptures of personal laws ofdiversity. Religion was initially created for the people to have a firm believer in almighty and asense of strong unambiguous force to govern, help and support the foots on the planet.

The motive of religion as mentioned before was not able to survive in the last few centuries as it hasbeen a strong hand in the upliftment of inequality and discrimination between people whichironically was created to abolish the same and promote the sense of humankind and humanity.The suppression of minorities by the majority or the ruling of minority and war cry of themajority is what religion should not be used for The Preamble of the Universal Declaration of Human Rights (UDHR) states clearly that "recognition of the inherent dignity and of the equal and inalienable rights of all members of the human family is the foundation of freedom,Justice and peace in the world.

It can be assumed that the issue of the Uniform Civil Code in India is a sensitive issue and requires much thought before it is adopted by the Indian state.

Is the clock ticking to the vivid adoption and acceptance of article 44 or are we still paving andmaking religion sit on the pedestal and mask on inequality and inhumane activities?

The Constitutional Fold

Article 44 of the Constitution of India requires the state to endeavor to guarantee a common Civil Code for its citizens across India. Secular activities, such as inheritance protected by personal laws, must be separated from religion. On the contrary, a uniform law so worked out and applied to all would promote national unity. The Common Civil Code would violate the fundamental right to religious freedom mentioned in Articles 25 and; second, it would amount to minority tyranny.

The first objection is false, because secular activity related to religious practiceis exempt from this guarantee. and since personnel laws (as argued from this point of view) relate to secular activities, they fail within the framework of the state's regulatory power. As for the second point, nowhere in advanced Muslim countries has the personal rights of any minority been recognized as so inviolable as to prevent the adoption of a civil code in Turkey and Egypt. Nominority is allowed to have such rights.

The term civil code is used to cover the entire body of laws that govern. Rights relating to property and other personal matters such as marriage, divorce, alimony, adoption and inheritance. As things are, there are Different laws that apply these aspects to different communities in India. Hence, the laws governing inheritance or divorceamong Hindus in would be different from those for Muslims or Christians, et cetera.

The term Civil Code is used to cover the entire set of laws on property rights and other laws in personal matters such as marriage, divorce, child support, adoption, and inheritance. Hence the laws governing inheritance or divorce among Hindus in would be different from those for Muslims or Christians, etc.

The leaders of India at the time wanted a secular constitution modelled on Western democracy. However, there was no secularism in the western sense, but a "secular" state with religious laws for its religious groups. Through threats from Islamists to keep Sharia law strictly unchanged. Hence, the Muslims and the Christians had to be governed by their own set of laws.

The effect of the Hindu marriage act was to prohibit polygamy amongst Hindus and to increase the right of divorced wife to maintenance or alimony. The act applied to everyone in India except Muslim, Christians,

Parsees and Jews. Since Jews and Parsees are a small minority remained de facto the only large community with a distinct religiouslaw that had not been reformed to reflect modern concepts. The legal practice of excluding Muslims continued with the passage of the dowry prohibition act of 1961 which specifically excluded, "dowry" or "mehr" in the case of persons to whom the Muslim personal law(shariat) applies".

In 1973 on a debate over the revision of the criminal procedure code, it was pointed outin regard to the maintenance of divorced wives that in cases involving Muslims, the court should take note as to whether the woman had received maintenance under the personal law. For Muslims this period is from iddah or 3 months after the divorce. While the period 1950- 1985 can be summarized as a period in which the Muslim personal laws of were exempt from legislation and were not reformed, it can also be seen as a period of in which secular avenues were opened to Muslims to the largest of that was the Special Marriage Act of 1954. The idea behind this law was to give anyone in India the opportunity to get married in outside of personal law, what we would call a civil marriage.

In many ways, Law was almost identical to the Hindu Marriage Law of 1955, which gives an idea of how secularized Law had become in relation to Hindus.

The Special marriage law allowed Muslims to marry under Law and thus to maintain their protection, which was generally beneficial for Muslim women, which was not to be found in personal law. Succession and instead of the respective Muslim personal law divorce is also regulated by secular law and the maintenance of a divorced wife would be based on the rules laiddown in civil law.

The Shah Bano case went to the Supreme Court on April 23, 1985, which ruled that the divorced Shah Bano was entitled to maintenance under Article 125 of the Code of Criminal Procedure (CrPC). The government of Rajeev Gandhi acted swiftly by passing the Muslim Women's Act of 1986, a law that essentially provided alimony for Muslim women outside the Penal Code, ensuring that Muslim women were not protected by the law that they could no longer fall back on Article 125 of the CrPC. Was an improvement over previous divorce rights under Sharia law or Muslim personal laws, which the Shah Bano deemed inadequate. Those who want to reform Muslim personal laws have often cited examples from Muslim countries that such reform is possible.

Tence Farais in his chapter 'The Development of Islamic Law', points out that the 1961 Ordinance on Pakistani Muslim Family Law "requires written approval from an arbitration board for a man who wants to marry a second wife". Appointed by the government". The interesting point about Pakistan is that India and Pakistan were ruled by Muslims under the Sharia law of 1937 from to 1947.However, by 1961, Pakistan, a Muslim country, had reformed its Muslim law more than India did in, and this is still the case today. The demand for a unified civil code essentially means unifying all these "personal laws" into a set of secular laws dealing with these issues that apply to all citizens of India regardless of the community to which they belong. Such a uniform code was not described in detail, it was supposed to contain the most modern and progressive aspects of all existing personal laws and discard the declining ones.

If you look at the countries in Europe that have civil codes, everyone who goes there from all over the world and all minorities have to adhere to the civil code, it doesn't feel tyrannical to the minority.

The main problem is to create national unity in this country. We believe we have national unity, but there are many factors and important factors that still seriously jeopardize our national consolidation. Communalism creates discrimination on two levels: on the one hand, between people of different religions, and on the other, between the two sexes. This dangerous and devastating effect should be eliminated in , possibly through the introduction of a uniform civil code. For women, who make up nearly half of India's population, the Uniform Civil Code provides equality and justice in the courts regardless of religion. in marriage, divorce, alimony, custody, inheritance, adoption, etc.

The only step taken in this direction was the codification of Hindu law, despite the great protest of; But the codification of Muslim law or the enactment of a common civil code is a sensitive issue because of its politicization.

Merits of UCC

If a Common Civil Code were promulgated and implemented: It would support and accelerate national integration; overlaps of legal provisions could be avoided; Decline in Human Rights Litigation in the World; The feeling of unity and the national spirit would be awakened, and thecountry would emerge with new strength and power to finally meet the defeats of the communal and diversionist forces. Israel, Japan, France and Russia are strong today because of their sense of togetherness, which we still have to develop and spread. India has set itself the ideal of a secular society, and in this context the realization of a unified civil code of becomes even more desirable, such a law will eliminate the diversity of marriage law of, simplify the Indian legal system and become the most homogeneous Indian society. It will separate law from religion, which is a highly desirable goal to achieve in a pattern of secular and socialist society. It will create a national identity and help curb the Fissiparous tendencies in the country. It will contain uniform provisions applicable to all and based on social justice and gender equality in family matters.

According to the Committee on the Status of Women in India: "The continuation of various personal laws that allow discrimination against men and women violates fundamental rights and the preamble of the Constitution, which promises to guarantee all citizens" equal rights and contradicts the spirit of natural integration.

In the committee recommended the rapid application of the constitutional directive in Article 44 through the adoption of a Single Civil Code in the realm of equality and diversity.

<u>**Criticism**</u>

- No urgency: the code is neither a priority nor an indispensable requirement for national integration The code is seen as a long-term social objective Some intellectuals believe that the implementation of the code must logically go through three stages:
- The first stage is the codification of the personal law of various notifications, so that over a period of time an adequate comparative legal basis is available, which serves as the basis for the principles of the uniform civil code. Transitional phase of optionality If the code conflicts with the personal laws of a community, the community in question should adopt an Exception received
- Operational problems: Ram Jethmalaini speaks in of a serious practical difficulty in adopting a uniform marriage law from most people - the Special Marriage Law of 1954 and preferring formal marriages. Religiously it is difficult, because the proponents of the Code of did not, in his opinion, give serious thought to what the different religious customs of in connection with marriage would look like and look like.
- It would not significantly improve India's democratic ideal: In Nepal, the introduction of a uniform civil code has not improved national integration. false It can be argued that a democracy can survive even

with the respect of separate personal laws of different communities, it depends on the specific historical experience of the nation and the structure of society, in fact, many democratic nations of the world today flourish without existence. a UCC

- Threat to minorities: Some see the code as a threat to their religious identityas the code will seek to amalgamate all people The historical abuse of power by majority communities results in minorities naturally diverging from later reforms, so if you so convincing everyone to be comfortable and accepting a civil uniform law will be a long and burning price in maybe one. which will end in failure.

Judicial Approach

The Supreme Court first ordered Parliament to organize a UCC in the case of Mohammad Ahmed Khan against Shah Bano Begum, popularly known as the Shah Bano case, in 1985, seeking assistance for her husband under Article 125 of the Code of Criminal Procedure after giving her Triple Talaq. She also claimed that Article 44 of the Constitution was still a dead letter.

The then Chief Justice of India, Y.V. Chandrachud stated, "A common civil code will help the cause of national integration by eliminating divergent allegiances to the law withconflicting ideologies"

After this decision, discussions, meetings and riots at the national level. The government led by Rajiv Gandhi overturned the decision in the Shah Bano case by Muslim Women's Law (Right to Protection in the Event of Divorce) of 198628, which restricted a Muslim woman's right to maintenance under Article 125 of the Code of Criminal Procedure. In,to enforce this bill, the Supreme Court merely made a remark to proclaim the UCC; are not binding on the government or parliament and that no interference with personal laws may take place, unless the demand comes from within. Mary Roy v. Kerala raised the question before the Supreme Court that certain provisions of the Travancore Christian Succession Act of 1916 were unconstitutional, under Art.14 Under those provisions, his widow would have a permanent wedlock in the event of death is only entitled to a terminable part of her life in the event of her death or remarriage and her daughter. It has also been argued in that the Travancore Act was superseded by the Indian Succession Act of 1925. The Supreme Court avoided examining whether the gender inequality in inheritance matters violated Article 14, but ruled that the Travancore Act was replaced by the Indian Succession Act. Mary Roy was described as a " momentary "decision towards ensuring gender equality on inheritance issues. Finally, the Supreme Court issued a directive for the Indian Union in Sarla Mudgal v Union of India that Indian leaders did not adhere to the theory of two nations or the theory of three " nations believed in and that therewould be only one nation in the Republic of India and no community could claim to remain the basis of religion in. However, it is worth noting what the Supreme Court expressed in the Lily Thomas case. The Supreme Court has no authority to issue instructions for the application of the Guiding Principles'.

Sinha and Justicia A.R. Lakshamanan cancelled the section and declared it unconstitutional. Chief Justice Khare stated, "We would like to note that Article 44 states that the state will endeavor to guarantee all citizens a unified civil code throughout India,deeply regrets that Article 44 of the Constitution has been enacted, The Parliament has yet to intervene to work out a common civil code in the country.

A common civil code will help the national integration cause by eliminating ideological contradictions". The court recently regrettedwhen hearing a case concerning whether a Christian had the right to bequeath goods to a charity that has not yet implemented a Unified Civil Code. This is not the first time the Supreme Court has spoken out in favor of a Unified Civil Code or had a bad opinion of the government and legislature's inability to say so other occasions, as in the case of Shah Bano case.

However, it should be borne in mind what the Supreme Court expressed in the Lily Thomas case.The Supreme Court has no authority to apply the Guiding Principles. Therefore, to overturn all arrests, it reiterates that the Supreme Court failed to issue instructions to codify a Common Civil Code in July 2003 when a Christian priest knocked on the doors of the Court of Justice to validate the constitutional validity of Section 118 of the Indian Succession Act to contest of Kerala, John Vallamatton filed a 1997 judicial petition finding that section 118 of that law discriminated against Christians for imposing undue restrictions on the voluntary donation of property to religious or charitable purposes.

Chief Justice Khare stated, "We would like to note that Article 44 states that the state shall endeavor to guarantee all citizens a uniform civil code throughout the territory of India".

<u>Amalgamating the Subject</u>

Rather than a top-down approach to a standalone code, prudence lies in a bottom-up approach to policy making through consensus building on uniformity. clear and unambiguous language in Chapter (Part IV) itself. The application of state policy in the legislative process forms the public order of India. Moreover, the same thing is mentioned in the constitution; the constitutionof the country.

Overall, it can also be read that the UCC was constituted as a public order that the state must follow for better governance, instead of deriving it in a code in the literal sense of the word in the middle (i.e., reducing) from the whirlwind of general concern; In the given context of vigilante justice followed by a recovery through the use of the stick in the literal senseof the word. Thus, despite its legal potential, codification cannot be enforced by the right-wing regime because it was supposed to defeat democracy; while it is a fundamental feature of the Constitution. From ancient times, as also mentioned above, even the greatest rulers like Asoka and Akbar did not resort to coercion to the point of imposing civil practices on their subjects; thesame can be interpreted as the cultural heritage of India. Under the given circumstances, the Unity Principle can slowly but steadily be introduced through amendments to the laws currently in force and not as a stand-alone legal act.

Cluster coding for uniformity instead of crocodiles cry out for a de novo code born with minority fire and fury will likely cope better with wandering patriarchs within a creed; with the same law of the land, albeitin pieces, used as a cane to domesticate them if necessary, so that the purpose and purpose of Codification of Article 44 of the Constitution can be achieved without recourse to legislative building blocks. and mortar for another room in the house, which is already crammed with statutes.

"By making countless statutes, people just confused you what God achieved in ten." The pure form of religious practices has been transformed into certain unorthodox religious practices that are unclean from cruel spirits"

Author's Bio

Myself Shreya Lal.

I am an ambitious undergraduate law school student of a reputed college and looking forward for experiences to whet my knowledge and proficiency regarded towards my skill. I am still tutoring myself towards various pavements of life and standing firm at all my decisions with immense dignity and inquisitiveness. I tend to do all work assigned to me with all travail and passion to the organisation significant.

CHAPTER THREE

AN ANALYSIS OF DOCTRINE OF LEGITIMATE EXPECTATION

Author: Soham Sinha, III year of B.B.A.,LL.B(Hons.) From Bennett University Greater Noida.

ABSTRACT

Promising something is not a single transaction its rather two ways. Promise is done with the intention that it is to be kept or acted upon by the other party. Similar is the case if we consider our administrative system. We the citizens have various expectations form the authorities and such is due to the promises kept and the practices undertaken in the past. But due to the presence of principle of delegated legislation, separation of power, promises which were kept rather goes against the people's expectation and thus they are deprived of advantage or benefits. To address this issue comes the Doctrine of Legitimate Expectation. This gives a form of legal help to the deprived people, rather they get the locus standi to challenge the action of the administration. This Doctrine do not come as a legal right, but it helps an individual to make the authority accountable in case of violation of certain duties. It also helps in ensuring that the authorities do not abuse their power, and such is prevented by the natural justice and the sense of fairness. The Doctrine exists as a Judicial safeguard for the individual deprived of benefit due to actions taken by the administration and such action taken is against the expectation of the public. Thus, this Doctrine allows the individual to challenge such deprivation, in a way upholding the principle of audi alteram partem.

The paper would be containing of a brief introduction of the Doctrine and its features. We would be looking into certain case laws which would signify the existence of the doctrine in England, followed by its origin and development in India. Next, we would look into who can apply the doctrine. We would also look upon the types of legitimate expectations which are procedural and substantive legitimate expectation and discuss about it. Next, we would look upon situations when the use of doctrine is formed. We will also discuss about relation between the Doctrine and Principle of Natural Justice Then we would discuss about the criticism of the doctrine. Lastly, will end with a conclusion and analysis of the Doctrine.

<u>INTRODUCTION</u>

Presently, there are promises to introduce various policies, programs, along with various assurances which are made by the government or the administrative authorities. Since it is made, general public gets an expectation that the said promises or assurances would be provided to them and eventually they would be benefitted through it. But there are various instances when the authorities deviate from their said promise and assurances and take different course of action which ultimately results in various losses and damages to the public. To cure or remedify the losses, the general public gets the opportunity to present their part of expectation which was assured by the authorities and later deprived off. Doctrine of Legitimate Expectation comes into picture in such cases as a tool or a Judiciary safeguard. The Doctrine is a domain of public law, which helps in providing relief or claims of the public on basis of law. Lord Denning in 1969, first used the term "Legitimate Expectation". The expectation as already stated may arise to general public due to an express statement, undertaking by the administrative authority or even through a practice which is generally practiced regularly. The term Legitimate expectation cannot be compared with general anticipation or even desires and hopes, rather it is a type of Principles of natural justice. Such expectation created is also protected by the courts through "fair play in action".

The Doctrine comes into play when it is shown by the public that due to the expectation, he/she has relied on it and if such expectation gets denied then he/she shall be deprived. Then if it is found that the decision made by the authority was gross, unreasonable, affecting the natural justice and also against the public interest, then only the court's intervention is required in such matters.

The Doctrine has several features. Firstly, public law allows to go to the court even there is no statutory violation, but because of deprived expectation where the grounds are legitimate. Public can claim not because of a legal claim but to make the administrative authority accountable for its action. Secondly, the Doctrine comes into existence due to the presence of Article 14 which demands for fairness in the actions of the administration. Scope of this Article is not only on class legislation which is arbitrary but also in if the state action is arbitrary. Thirdly, the expectation needs to be legitimate and for the public interest.

ORIGIN AND DEVELOPMENT OF DOCTRINE IN ENGLAND

The expression was developed firstly in England in 1969 through the case of Schmidt v. Secretary of State for Home Affairs. The case showed that even though a foreigner was deprived of entering in UK, he should get the minimum right of being heard. He also had the legitimate expectation to be allowed to stay and that to for the allotted time. Later cases also saw the use of the principle without actually mentioning or expressly stating the terms. One of such case was Regina v. Liverpool Corporation ex parte Liverpool Taxi Fleet Operators Association , where without the knowledge of the taxi operator association, the licenses of taxi were increased, and such was held as unjustified as it was a general expectation on the part of the association.

Another landmark case of England could be the case of A.G. Of Hong Kong v. Ng Yuen Shiu. The court stated that it is the duty of the public authority to follow the procedures and take actions which are fair. Court also distinguished between expectation and anticipation where expectation can be considered as legitimate if there is the presence of sanctions, procedures which are legal along with customs which are generally followed. Since there is no "crystallised right" for legitimate expectation, there is the absence of direct relief. Legitimate expectation offers the right of fair hearing in case where the promise or assurance by the administration was withdrawn negatively. The administration in this case has to justify its decision and it should be free of arbitrariness, unreasonableness and taken in interest of public. The court gets the power of judicial review, but such scope gets limited when the issue at hand is regarding policy changes. In such cases, the court is expected to refrain from interfering.

ORIGIN AND DEVELOPMENT OF DOCTRINE IN INDIA

In India, the Doctrine got its exposure in the case of State of Kerala v. K.G. Madhavan Pillai. The case arose due to a sanction which provided to upgrade as well as open existing and new schools respectively. But later the sanction was suspended. On being challenged, the court stated that the respondents had the right claim of legitimate expectation due to the sanction which was already passed. Also, the later order passed was going against the principles of natural justice. Legitimate expectation not only arises in case of promises or sanctions but it arises even due to a constant practice. This was witnessed in the case of Navjyoti Coop. Group Housing Society v. Union of India. The issue was regarding deciding seniority with respect to allotment of land. Old policy decided seniority on the basis of the date on which registration was made. Later new policy was introduced which decided seniority on the basis of the approval date in the final list. The apex court in this matter stated that the continuous practice through the old policy entitled the people in the housing societies to legitimate expectation. Authority can pass a new policy but that should not be against the legitimate expectation and if it is against the doctrine, such should be made in interest of public. The court also stated that going against the expectation, or even the continuous practice in existence comes under the category of fairness. But in the case in hand, opportunity though a public notice regarding the same was not provided to the housing societies. It was also stated in the case of UOI v. Hindustan Development Corporation that Legitimate expectation comes into play even when the person actually do not have the legal right, but due to the doctrine the person can be treated in the same fashion. In this case, the doctrine was majorly related to procedural legitimate expectation (will be discussed later). The doctrine allows the individual to have fair hearing before any decision in negative or positive sense is undertaken.

WHO CAN APPLY THE DOCTRINE OF LEGITIMATE EXPECTATION?

The doctrine can only be invoked by those who have dealings, transactions, or agreements with an authority, on which such established practice bears, or those who have a recognised legal relationship with the authority. The doctrine of legitimate expectation cannot be used by a total stranger who has no connection with the authority, nor had single prior dealings with the authority and have never entered into any transaction or agreements with the authority. They cannot simply invoke the doctrine because the authority has a general duty to behave reasonably.

TYPES OF LEGITIMATE EXPECTATION

Legitimate Expectation can be of two types, Procedural and substantive legitimate expectation.

PROCEDURAL LEGITIMATE EXPECTATION

In this form, it is expected of the authority to follow certain procedures before they produce their decision. Proper procedure means consulting, enquiring, hearing the parties before giving the decision. The main aim of this form is to make sure that the actions taken by the administration are free from arbitrariness, self-serving and giving respect to the parties who would be affected in a sense by the decision they make. All such would imply that natural justice is maintained taking into consideration the fairness of decision by the administration. Situations of such form arise in case an individual expects of a certain policy but provided with something different, or a pre-existing policy which was expected was not applied in the present scenario. Other situations may be, individuals expected of a benefit due to norms by the administration but such was deprived off due to changes in norms or due to different decision of authority which was actually not promised in the early stage. The Doctrine comes in play in such situations only to give the affected people a right to be heard because of the legitimate expectation they had from the administration.

SUBSTANTIVE LEGITIMATE EXPECTATION

The substantive form of doctrine is still under formation in India. It actually provides individual with benefit which is substantial, and such arises because of the legitimate expectation such individual had. This form of legitimate expectation was seen in use in the case of R v. Secretary of state for the Home department, ex parte Khan. It was found that mere change in policy wont attract the doctrine unless previous consultations were not undertaken. It is upto the court to decide whether interest of public should be given importance. Later in the case of R v. North and East Devon Health Authority, ex parte Coughlan certain situations which may arise were discussed. In case the promise made by the authority was a type of contract, court would look into the case and decide whether depriving the expectation can be considered as an abuse of power. In other situation of policy change, the court would look into the rationality of the decision made and see whether consequences of the decision made were with prior investigation.

SITUATIONS DEMANDING THE FORMATION OF LEGITIMATE EXPECTATION

In the early stages, certain situations were enunciated in the case of Madras City Wine Merchants v. State of Tamil Nadu regarding forming legitimate expectation. Firstly, presence of promise or representation expressly by the administration. Secondly, ambiguous and unclear promises should not be entertained. Thirdly, any pre-existing policies or practices which are expected by the public to operate in the present. There are also cases when the doctrine would have no role in situation a particular authority has the power under executive policy to make decisions and there would be no restrictions to introduce any new policy which is actually required in the interest of public as a whole. It was also cleared in the case of M.P. Oil Extraction v. State of M.P , that in appropriate instances, the doctrine of legitimate expectations works in the field of public law and is regarded a substantial and enforceable right. In this case, the concerned industry had legitimate expectation that the agreements would be extended in a similar manner, based on historical practise and the renewal clause.

Situations when the Doctrine can be or cannot be exercised was clearly enumerated in the case of GNCT of Delhi v. Naresh Kumar. Firstly, the safeguard of doctrine of legitimate expectation present with the citizen do not arise as an enforceable right, but if such expectation of citizen is given lack of importance or any arbitrary decision is made regarding such expectation then this would deem to be an invalid decision. Secondly, the doctrine comes in existence when there is any promise made expressly by the authority, or due to any continuous practice expected to continue because of an existing policy and all such expectations should be reasonable in nature. Thirdly, the doctrine would be attracted, if the authority provides any decision depriving individuals of their expected benefit. Such decision can be considered valid if rational grounds for taking such decision were communicated prior to the individuals. Fourthly, proper public notice or fair hearing were provided to the individuals before such decision is implemented. Fifthly, it would be court's ambit to look into the changes made by the authority and decide whether such is against the legitimate expectation, irrational, or a decision a reasonable person could never have made.

DOCTRINE OF LEGITIMATE EXPECTATION AND PRINCIPLES OF NATURAL JUSTICE

Both the doctrines of legitimate expectation and natural justice has to be read or considered together. Every actions of the state should comply with Article 14 of the Constitution and where the concept of non-arbitrariness is an important factor. In such a case, a citizen's mere fair or legitimate expectation may not be a distinct enforceable right, but if there is failure to recognize and provide due importance to it might help in making the decision arbitrary, and this is how the importance of a legitimate expectation is part of the concept of non-arbitrariness, a required aspect of the rule of law. Any reasonable expectation is a relevant factor that must be taken into account to provide a just decision-making process. It must also be noted that whenever such question comes into consideration, the public interest in a larger sense should be considered. The condition would be satisfied if the public authority made a genuine decision and in this way a guarantee of non-arbitrariness and the ability to have a judicial scrutiny would be established. Thus, in this way the doctrine of legitimate expectation is considered into the rule of law and exists in our legal system in this way. In a rule of law society, the main objective of the expectation is that those in higher positions of power and authority must be able to publicly justify their actions as legally valid, socially sensible, and just. In such conditions, the public's right to protect themselves from abuse of discretion becomes an inherent right in a democracy. They must not succumb to the fatal tentacles of arbitrary and unjustified reasons or decisions.

CRITICISM OF THE DOCTRINE

The procedural aspect of Legitimate expectation is used in a liberal sense in India because of maintaining natural justice of fairness and right to be heard in the civil administration. The Substantive aspect of the doctrine has failed to stand on its own because it is used mainly as an addition to other claims mainly the doctrine of promissory estoppel which helps in protecting a promisee by enforcing the promise, he /she entered into without taking into consideration it was a contract or not. The problem of it can be clearly understood through the case of Lalaram v. Jaipur Development Authority. The applicants in this case had the expectation of compensation from Supreme Court in form of land. This expectation was denied by the Government, who claimed such promise was against the business rule set in Rajasthan. Later court made the government accountable for denying amending a policy as the rule was found to be unsustainable for the purpose of interpreting it out of context. This was possible by invoking doctrine of promissory estoppel along with substantive legitimate expectation as a supplement. Justice was granted through this judgement but there was absence of clarity because legitimate expectation was mixed with reasonable expectations and still was distinguished as an equitable notion. Various other cases saw the substantive legitimate expectation but none of it were enforced as it was found out to be not substantive and presence of legitimate expectation was not found. This could have been avoided if the doctrine is allowed to stand on its own as a distinct standard of public law rather than as a supplement to promissory estoppel and thus would be used as an effective safeguard against the unlawful or arbitrary decisions of the administration.

CONCLUSION

The requirement of scrutiny in every matter is quite a effective way of undergoing, similarly laws needs to be under scrutiny. Any administrative decisions made needs to be fair and as per the expectations of the public. If the decisions are not following the expectations, individuals gets the safeguard of Doctrine of legitimate expectation for ensuring a good administration system. With the existence of various laws, this doctrine comes as guardian to the individuals. There isn't a comprehensive list of expectations of the public, and such is not a flaw in the legal system. The doctrine is supposed to correspond to the limitless list of public expectations and wishes.. The doctrine cannot be exercised merely as a right but can be used in case the legitimate expectation denied is going against Article 14 of the Constitution. The courts have been adopting a more active role in policing the use of discretionary power and maintaining the rule of law, while acknowledging that going against the Executive is appropriate in some circumstances. As a result, the courts must strike a balance between permissible judicial involvement and judicial interference that violates the separation of powers norm. Maintaining this balance will become increasingly important as the concept of legitimate expectations develops

<u>Author's Bio</u>

I am Soham Sinha a student of 3rd year BBA-LLB of college Bennett University, Greater Noida. I am thankful to the editor for selecting my article for the purpose of publication.

CHAPTER FOUR

UNIFORMITY IN LEGAL DRINKING AGE IN INDIA

Author: Bhagesh Gupta, III year of B.A.,LL.B from manipal university jaipur.

<u>Introduction</u>

Alcohol usage, the legal drinking age in India, and the consistency of the legal drinking age in India have all been contentious issues in India. According to a recent estimate, India's per capita alcohol consumption has more than quadrupled between 2016 and 2020. Despite alcohol prohibitions in several places across the country, over 88 percent of Indians under the age of 25 purchase or use alcoholic drinks. According to India's present alcohol regulations, each state has the authority to make its own rules. This has caused a lot of uncertainty among Indian inhabitants, as well as a lot of diversity. On the one hand, we talk about "Unity in Diversity yet on the other hand, there exist disparities in alcohol consumption among inhabitants of different states. According to present alcohol rules, a person of 21 years of age can legally consume alcohol in Jharkhand today, but if that same person travels to Delhi or Bihar tomorrow, he will be considered an unlawful drinker. The need for uniformity in legal drinking across the country is urgent, and it is a critical component in limiting the breadth of discrimination and other bad aspects of it. Finally, alcohol has become a need rather than a luxury, and it must be dealt with urgently. One of the most thrilling aspects of a person's life is their first time drinking or tasting an alcoholic beverage. Alcohol is a toxin that may be both poisonous and addicting. It is generated when yeast ferments the carbohydrates in grains, fruits, and vegetables to produce ethanol (ethyl alcohol). Everyone enjoys the rush of adrenaline that comes with being old enough to drink what he's seen his elders ingest. However, every government imposes various limits on the usage of alcohol, one of which is a minimum drinking age. In India, alcohol usage has long been a hot topic. In India, it has long been a contentious topic. The non-uniformity in India's legal drinking age has sparked a discussion among millennials. In India, the legal drinking age varies from state to state. India is the only country in the world where states have the authority to enact alcohol laws, resulting in varying legal drinking ages across the country.

While some governments advocate for a full prohibition on its usage for consumption, others set an age limit for alcohol consumption. There are legal purchasing ages for beer, wine, and sprits both on and off premises, as well as by kind of beverage (beer, wine, and sprits). According to Merriam Webster, drinking age is defined as the age at which a person can lawfully purchase and consume alcohol. India, too, maintains such limits on the purchase and use of alcoholic beverages. However, the imposition in India is not uniform across the country. We have a standard legal age for marriage driving, and voting but we don't have a uniform legal drinking age. List 2(Entry 51 and 54) of the Seventh Schedule of the Indian Constitution has granted State authorities the right to amend and control alcohol laws in their nation, resulting in a non-uniform legal drinking age throughout the world.

Also Article 4710 of the Indian Constitution gives each state the authority to enforce the ban of intoxicating beverages and narcotics. As a result, each Indian state has its unique alcohol usage and buying rules. While some Indian states have an age limit of 18, others have outright outlawed it or have a specific prohibition up to a particular age. This research paper will discuss why a uniform legal drinking age is necessary and why it is the right thing to do.

Current Alcohol Laws In India

In India, the legal age for purchasing and drinking alcoholic drinks varies by state. In certain states, alcohol use is completely outlawed, while in others, the legal drinking age ranges from 18 to 25. It is because the issue of alcohol is covered under Entry 51 of the State List of the VII Schedule of the Indian Constitution. This allows all states to make their own laws about the present topic. This has resulted in significant diversity, with varying legal drinking ages in different states. Article 47 of the Indian Constitution, which was enacted following debates in the Constituent Assembly, is a directive principle of state policy that is supremely fundamental for the country's governance. It grants the state complete discretionary privilege over the consumption of liquor as a beverage, despite the fact that it is integrally hazardous to humanoid health.

Not only does the state have the authority to control consumption, but it also has the authority to put limits and prohibitions on the commerce and business of alcoholic beverages. As a result, a citizen has no essential right to trade or do commercial in liquor as a brew, and actions that are res additional commercium cannot be approved out by any inhabitant, and the State-run can completely forbid trade or do commercial in transportable liquor, as well as generate a monopoly in the trade or commercial of liquor. The state-run can also place limits and prohibitions on the trade or business of liquor and beverages, which are inherently distinct from those compulsory on the trade or commercial of authorised doings and res commercium commodities and apprenticeships. Kandahar Distillers vs. State of Kerala, AIR 2013 SC 1812. As a result, the legal drinking age in India varies.

Alcohol Policy World Wide

In all of the other nations, the legal drinking age is the same. Either it is banned, or there are no limitations, or there is no set age, but it is standard for that country. Alcohol is outlawed in Afghanistan, Argentina has an 18-year-old drinking age, and Cambodia has no legal drinking age. There is a standard legal drinking age in the rest of the countries as well. Nepal, a neighbouring Asian nation, has set the drinking age at 24 years old, whereas China and Singapore, farther north, have set the drinking age at 18 years old. In Japan and South Korea, the minimum drinking age has been set at 20 and 19, respectively. Drinking is illegal in most Islamic nations; however, non-Muslims residing in Pakistan above the age of 21 are permitted to drink alcoholic beverages.

Almost all African countries, with the exception of Egypt and Sudan, consider 18 to be the legal drinking age. Argentina, Brazil, Venezuela, Cuba, Russia, Ukraine, Latvia, Lithuania, Czech Republic, France, Republic of Ireland, Poland, Slovenia, and Slovakia are among the Latin American, Oceanian, and European countries that have set the drinking age at 18. In Austria, Germany, Belgium, and the Netherlands, a purchaser of wine or beer must be 16 years old, and a purchaser of spirits must be 18 years old. In the European countries of Italy and Portugal, 16-year-olds can buy wine, drink it, and even work in a wine shop. The minimum drinking age in Scandinavian nations, with the exception of Denmark, is set at 18, however these privileges are only valid until the age of 20. In Iceland and Sweden, purchases of alcoholic drinks must be at least 20 years old, while those aged 18 and 19 are permitted to consume. Finland and Norway allow 18-year-olds to enjoy lighter, less concentrated beverages, whereas 21-year-olds can consume highly concentrated drinks. In Denmark, the legal age for purchasing alcohol containing 1.2 to 16.5 percent alcohol is 16 years old in shops and 18 years old in restaurants and bars, while drinking and possessing alcohol is lawful at any age.

<u>Why Is It Necessary To Be Consistent?</u>

Because of the non-uniformity in India's legal drinking age, residents from all over the world face significant issues and disadvantages.

Smuggling

It is a well-known truth that if a person is encouraged or prohibited not to do something, the likelihood of performing that thing increases dramatically. The same may be said with alcohol. Even outlawing alcohol use hasn't proven to be a significant step in reducing alcohol usage. Indeed, the rate of liquor smuggling has increased as a result of this. The state's borders are trafficked with a large volume of booze. Foreign liquors produced in India were smuggled inside the Rajdhani Express in 2018. Despite repeated statements that the use, sale, and exchange of booze in the state is forbidden, drivers, attendants, and personnel have recently been discovered carrying whiskey bottles in trains in dry Bihar. Furthermore, since the new State Excise Act went into effect, over 1.2 lakh persons have been detained and over 6 lakh gallons of liquor have been seized. Dholpur police officers seized 2,500 cartons of booze from two lorries travelling to Gujarat on the national route.

Black Marketing

It is hard to limit someone in this day of variety. When a person has a different way to absorb things, he will naturally gravitate toward it and become reliant on it. It is the nation's responsibility to guarantee that the law's loopholes are closed. In an ideal world, if the drinking age is the same in all states, there will be less likelihood of liquor smuggling. Respecting the governments that have prohibited consumption on religious and state moral grounds, the police must guarantee that the smuggling rate decreases. The universality of drinking age will apply in states where there is now a large disparity in drinking ages.

Discrimination between the citizens of different state

As we all know, the legal drinking age is not universal and differs from state to state. The problem is real, and it has to be addressed. A similar sort of person may be found all around the country. Although the economic and social aspects differ, they collectively reflect a single country. On the one hand, the non-uniformity of the legal drinking age discriminates amongst persons. According to the existing legislation, an 18-year-old in Uttar Pradesh is additional accountable than an 18-year-old in Delhi, but this is not the case. Article 14 of the Indian constitution states unequivocally that "the State must not refuse to any individual equality before the law or equal protection of the laws within its jurisdiction."

Furthermore, the sole basis for discrimination is that it must be positive discrimination that is based on reasonable reason and discernible differences. Indeed, why is there non-uniformity in the case of alcohol while the ability to vote and the right to drive have a uniform legal age across the country? When other issues of national importance have uniform ages, the logic cannot be applicable for the non-fixed scenario. Voting is a prudential topic for the country because it selects the entire political kingdom, however driving is one of the most significant issues within the realm of national security. If these two topics, which are far more important than drinking, have a standard age, then the right to drink should also have a fixed legal age across the country.

<u>Conclusion</u>

I also performed a questionnaire study on the subject, and I was surprised to discover that 80% of my respondents were unaware that different states in India have varying legal ages. The majority of people say it is set at 18, while some believe it is set at 21. The disadvantages of non-uniformity have outweighed the benefits. I believe that there should be an age restriction for drinking, but it should be standardised. India is one of the countries where about half of the population consumes alcohol. There is an essential need for a national policy to restrict liquor use. The nation has a responsibility to protect the public's health and to guarantee that article 21 or any of the rights are not violated in any way. Liquor has evident negative effects, and if legislators do not establish a regulating strategy, the residents of the city would suffer. India would undoubtedly sink into the abyss. Alcohol is currently a state topic, yet there is a clear need for federal intervention in this area. An hour is required for a uniform legal drinking age. As India celebrates its diversity, it must be protected, and laws dealing with the most important issues, such as the right to vote, the accurate to drive, and the right to marry, must be under the control of the central government for better and more robust regulation. The right to consume alcohol should also have a uniform age, and there is a need for a national policy that addresses all alcohol-related laws.

CHAPTER FIVE

HOW BLOCKCHAIN TECHNOLOGY CAN BE BOON FOR LEGAL WORLD

Author: Alpesh Kumar, III year of B.A.,LL.B(Hons.) From Chanakya National Law University.

Co-author: Shifali Gautam, IV year of B.A.,LL.B(Hons.) From Gujarat National Law University.

ABSTRACT

Blockchain technology is rapidly evolving and has the potential to disrupt every sector on the planet. Blockchain, which is well-known for its capacity to store data in a transparent and immutable ledger, provides organizations with a better degree of accuracy. The legal industry is likewise aiming to use distributed ledger technology to transform its business. It is therefore evident that blockchain technology is increasingly being used and is hence gaining acceptance despite the issues it carries with itself. This research paper will hus discuss the same in detail.

Keywords: Blockchain, technology, ledger, transaction, security.

INTRODUCTION

Blockchain, the technology that underpins Bitcoin, may be characterized as an open, distributed ledger that efficiently and permanently records transactions between users. Bitcoin is a subset of Blockchain technology, which is essentially a distributed multi-party ledger. It has the potential to improve the efficiency with which online transactions are conducted, comparable to the characteristics of other emerging technologies that aid in communication speed. Despite the pessimistic predictions, there is evidence that blockchain is a capable, innovative technology that will transform the way people deal, owing to its capacity to ensure confidence between unknown parties, protect data immutability, and eliminate the need for intermediaries. The benefits of Blockchain might be applied in supply chain management in the manufacturing, E-commerce, digital health, aviation, and retail sectors due to the possibility of smart contracts. As a result, the Blockchain architecture has the potential to revolutionize how companies and contracts are conducted. Although Blockchain allows for tamper-proof, verifiable, and transparent transactions, the underlying characteristics of decentralization have the potential to generate instability and upheaval in the present economic system. The bulk of governments have mostly ignored Blockchain technology's emergence. With its growing popularity, all legal regimes must determine if regulatory control of its usage is necessary, and if so, how to strike a balance between the Blockchain and the traditional system. Blockchains such as Bitcoin and Ethereum are well-known examples. Anyone may connect to the blockchain and conduct transactions on it. Anyone may operate a node on their computer and download a copy of Bitcoin, Ethereum, and other blockchains for free. In such situation, you may make money by participating as a block verifier (also known as a miner) and confirming transactions transmitted across the network by other users. Currently, a lawyer's responsibilities include gathering evidence in support of a client's viewpoint and utilizing that evidence to develop a logical argument. By automating the collection of evidence, blockchain may facilitate the streamlining of this procedure. For instance, instead of searching for data from many sources, conforming companies and institutions may send it directly to the attorneys. Open ledgers, like as Bitcoin, are accessible to all parties for inspection, and this openness may be very beneficial in situations of financial crime.

FEATURES OF BLOCKCHAIN TECHNOLOGY

The properties of Blockchain that characterize it as a game-changing and disruptive technology are as follows:

Trust

A new block in the ledger may only be created if the transaction is approved by a majority of the network participants, as indicated in the procedure. Only once the ledger has verified that the information exchanged is cryptographically secure is this agreement formed. The data is updated and distributed across network members, making it worthy of trust.

Transparency

A worldwide supply chain that uses blockchain technology may see an increase in transaction accuracy. Pricing monitoring systems and improved product distribution transparency might both benefit from the smart contract established using Blockchain technology. Real-time authentication is possible with blockchain, which might improve the long-term viability of the manufacturing process. Increased engagement in governance and decision-making might result from increasing the level of openness to the public.

Immutability

The data on the Blockchain that is connected to the prior ledger cannot be changed, modified, or lost. A permanent and incorruptible record is created as a result of this method. An auditable ledger keeps track of all changes, guaranteeing complete transparency.

No need of a central regulatory authority

No one individual, central mediator, or government maintains the ledger database, which is open to all network members. As a result, the ledger transaction between the two parties may be verified without the need for a central authority. Therefore, the ability to issue money is "decentralized," which is a revolutionary development.

Secure Operation

There has been an increase in public awareness of the risks of data security in conventional internet databases after the Cambridge Analytica affair. Governments across the globe have enacted strict data privacy rules, one of which being the European Union's GDPR (General Data Protection Regulation). Regulated guarantees alone can't address the problem of data security. This is when the Blockchain steps in to fill in the details that are missing. The encryption mechanism used to transfer information on the blockchain provides more security. As a result, it is an excellent choice for keeping highly confidential data, such as personal information.

<u>BLOCKCHAIN AND LEGAL FRATERNITY</u>

The Global Legal Blockchain Consortium wants to decentralize law, and blockchain might help. 70% of law firms surveyed by PwC expected to adopt smart contracts for transactional legal services in 2017. 41% of legal firms will utilize blockchain for transactional legal services, 21% for business support, and 31% for high-value legal services. Blockchain may help the legal profession create immutable, transparent databases. These might simplify smart contracts, mergers, and other transactions. Blockchain might make the legal sector more accessible by using digital signatures and smart contracts. It may cut legal costs, making it more affordable. It has the ability to promote industry transparency by offering an open, accessible database (ledger) to all stakeholders at all times. Blockchain might minimize administrative labor, leading to more cost-effective corporations. Blockchain will automate the legal system. Prefabricated smart contracts and other facilities might save lawyers time and money on administrative tasks. NITI Ayog recommended implementing blockchain into the judicial system in "Blockchain: The India Strategy Part I."

The legal field may benefit from Blockchain in the following ways:

- Smart Agreements: Traditional contracting procedures are paper-based, time-consuming, and error-prone. Smart contracts would be available online, using AI and biotechnology databases, simplifying a lawyer's work.
- Chain of Responsibility: Evidence gathering is crucial to any investigation. Keeping evidence on hand may be time-consuming and error prone. Storing a lot of evidence may be tough. Making evidence easily accessible in case of a long-term dispute may be an issue again. Keeping the chain of custody online, on an immutable, transparent, and secure platform, is more practicable. When forensics obtains crime scene evidence, it may be uploaded as a block to a chain and accessed immediately. Finally, evidence custodians have quick access to forensic findings and analysis.
- IP: IP filing, like ordinary contracts, is time-consuming and may need several administrative duties. Approval times may be decreased, and necessary resources can be delivered using blockchain technology. This may also be done in a supposedly straightforward manner:

1. Content makers register on the site and provide government-approved personal information.
2. After signing up, content providers may create an intellectual property for which they intend to submit a patent and then publish the details about their IP on the blockchain network.
3. Consumers of content may log in to the site and request IP access. In this instance, content producers may provide a smart contract and request payment.
4. Legal experts might assist in resolving any potential conflicts.

- Conflict and Settlement: Using a blockchain-enabled litigation app, a plaintiff might first login and provide his personal information and complaints to the blockchain-based litigation app. When they're ready, they may use the app to find specialized legal counsel and make contact with them. Email or text messages are used to notify both sides of the lawsuit, which is subsequently filed. It's possible for the defendant to use the app to get a lawyer, just like the prosecution. There are no papers or contracts that can be tampered with since the blockchain is immutable. Finally, a judge has the ability to view the time-stamped records of information and resolve disagreements between the parties involved in the lawsuits.
- Corporate documents: Blockchain technology records every company record and transaction on an immutable, secure, and transparent platform. These documents will be accessible eternally as blocks and may be accessed at any moment without attorneys' management.
- Criminal cases: According to a study released by The Police Foundation in the United Kingdom, blockchain might improve the criminal justice system's burdensome paperwork in the following ways:

1. Information would be more accessible to the general population.
2. Viewing permissions may be established at different levels.
3. The papers would have an auditable trail of modifications.
4. Interested parties might get quick updates.
5. The accuracy of records would be considerably improved.
6. As more data is made available to the public, a "glass government" is emerging.

- Document notarization: The process of notarizing a document ensures its proper execution by validating its legitimacy. Because blockchain technology uses timestamps and hashes to record transactions, it may make document notarization easier. Companies that provide notarization services may quickly establish the presence of a document by employing time stamps.
- Land Registries and Title Deeds: Blockchain simplifies land ownership paperwork. It might improve brokers' record transparency, update, and security. All government property data will be on the blockchain by 2020, according to the Dubai Blockchain Strategy. Cook County, Illinois established a blockchain pilot program in 2016 and successfully

implemented it in May 2017.

- ODR: Commercial arbitration is a low-cost, rapid, and private option. Using blockchain technology, ODR systems might provide secure cross-border and international dispute resolution. With many nations embracing blockchain ODR, it's logical to expect future courts to be more cost-effective in settling commercial conflicts. The Aragon Court agreed to allow users to report complaints or serve as jurors. Proposal Agreements are originally handled by the Aragon Court, but the underlying technology has the potential to arbitrate any two-way issue. Jur, Kleros, Doges, and Oath are all similar systems.
- Roles in Blockchain Workforce for Lawyers: Any new idea creates jobs. Blockchain might produce occupations like 'smart contract programmer/auditor' in the legal field.

<u>CONCLUDING REMARKS</u>

The technology of distributed ledgers Blockchain has the potential to transform the current world, making it a gift to humanity. Despite its frightening nature, the Blockchain, like the early days of the Internet, has the potential to alter governmental supervision. The necessity of the hour is to create legal frameworks that will enable Blockchain technologies to flourish. Blockchain might help regulators keep track of specific activity and verify legal compliance. It might be utilized in financial markets, AML compliance, market manipulation monitoring, and other industries by assessing cryptographic verifiability. Blockchain is the most revolutionary technology since the Internet. Smart contracts, corporate filings, criminal cases, dispute resolution, document notarizations, industry associations, intellectual property rights, land registries and property deeds, law firm operations, and public service records will be affected by transformation. All these involve lawyers. Both clients and attorneys should be tech-savvy. A lawyer may use blockchain to further a client's interests by exploring novel legal applications.

CHAPTER SIX

DOWRY DEATH IN INDIA

Author: Madhumita L, II Year of B.A.,LL.B from Christ University School of Law Bengaluru.

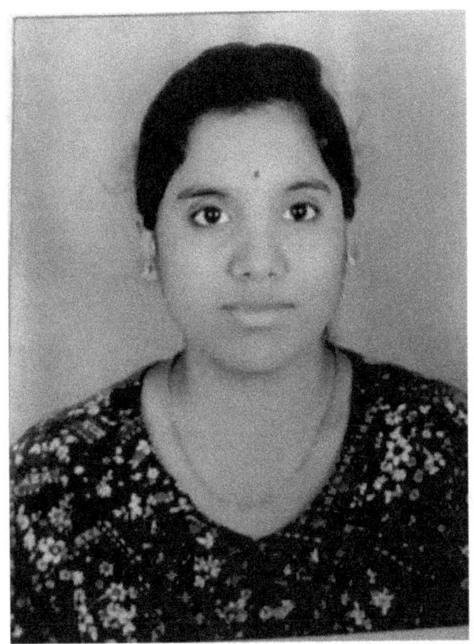

ABSTRACT

Human beings evolution is slow process where advanced stage was erect man was evolved which we call them as " Homo Sapiens" and then the gradual changes has come and gender and sex was looked,where gender is what society looks at and sex is the biological factor which is generally looked through. In India the customs was given due importance and in this note from the ancient period till today the women were suppressed for their gender and our society began to under spoken about women and began to torture her and then various customs like Sati, Dowry began,Then during British the sati was abolished and the age old Dowry and dowry death still happening in this 21st century society, laws has been advocated to curb this social evil.

STATEMENT OF PROBLEM

India is one such country where crimes against women are high, and in that dowry. The social reformers during the British period have taken a lot of pain to curb these social issues, for instance, the contribution of Raja Rammohan Roy, who, with the help of Lord William Benthick, abolished the sati system in India and but people did not think rationally,so still this type of crimes such as rape, dowry death and bride burning prevails in our society, The legal framework is progressive where the dowry prohibition act 1961 was implemented. In section 304 B, which discusses the essentials of dowry death, So this act is meant only for women. It prohibits giving or taking of dowry. Before this act came, the act was amended twice and the act mainly serves the purpose that women should not be demanded by dowry.but the major flaw in this act is it is vague in nature,influence of cultural aspect of women. Laws are not constant, it changes as the society moves forwards.so the necessary steps have been taken for the women's safety.

RESEARCH METHODOLOGY

The methodology adopted by the researcher is a doctrinal form of research. It is elaborate in nature where it gives a broad outlook on dowry death which is the prevalent social issue. It has analysed the issue of dowry death in three time periods also,Ancient, Medieval and Modern. The primary sources of research include legislations, case laws, various reports of international conventions, policies and rules formed by the government. The secondary sources include books, research articles, blogs, and various websites on this issue.The researcher has tried to figure out the suggestion to overcome these social issues. The researcher used the following keywords: the information regarding the research , the history of the dowry issues in India, the present legal analysis on the dowry death issue, the flaw in the act, the role of the government, and methods to prohibit dowry death.

Dowry death is one of the crimes against women, and it is an evil public issue , but still it is being practised. The concept of dowry has been there from the beginning, which can be noticed in the epics of Ramayana, where it is been said that Sita's father gave high weightage of dowry in marriage to Ram. Also, in Mahabharat, the dowry practice is witnessed where the queen of Pandavas, Draupadi brought dowry from her kingdom, horses and jewels and property were given in the marriage and Subhadra and Uttara. They brought dowry in the form of elephants and gold ornaments. But paradoxically queen Draupadi who wanted to marry Arjuna alone, but her wish was not fulfilled and she was harassed by Kauravas and her husbands remained silent as they lost the ludo game.The daughter of Sun who had a treasure box and she carried this as dowry to her husband Soma's place. In India during the medieval period there was a practice in which the father had to give the gift in the form of cash or ornaments to bride grooms and it was given for the security of their daughters in the paternal house. So this shows the role of money in marriage.The issue of dowry was slowly made mandatory by British rule and the main causes for the dowry death which is increasing day by day is due to the patriarchal society, especially in India where there is belief in the rigorous practice of the old customs and traditions,Then marriages were mostly decided by the parents, the consent of bride and bride grooms were not asked. The concept of dowry is done in different names like VaraDakshina and Kanyadan where the bride's father gives his daughter to his son in law and stridhan is the gift.

This cruel concept of dowry is spreading like a virus, where every family be it lower middle class till elite class makes sure that dowry should be given. So this has become a stigma and this practise has made the life of the bride's parents miserable and they would be in debt, which can lead to the poverty level. In India, the dowry rates differ based on the education qualification and beauty is given much priority. The dowry which has eventually raised and has led to major crimes against women is Dowry death or bride burning. This has been spoken and discussed in various platforms and debates, and this also raised the suicide rates of girls were in a family; three girls in the city of Kanpur committed suicide. The core reason is not to create any financial burden to their family as the father earned only 4000 per month, and with this money, he could not tolerate the expense of the older daughter. Thus India developing country is making efforts to remove "Dowry death" by legislative measures.

Dowry death in connection with demand for dowry and its effect on brides and their family - In India, it is a man dominated society. So the crimes against women are drastically high. In that Dowry death is the social issue that is affecting the bride's family. Firstly, as soon as they are born, the girl children are treated as a boon to the family because the girls go to the paternal family after marriage and even if she works, her income would not come to their parents. So the bride's family think that they will not get any return, and during the marriage, they face the dowry issue and get tensed like how much they will demand. Meanwhile, some women will still be harassed if she goes to in-laws for not satisfying the dowry they have taken at the time of marriage. Subsequently, the dowry death cases rapidly rose, in the case of Shanti vs state of Haryana, which deals with the demanding of the dowry after marriage where the Kailash was married to Sat pal and his mother subjected to torture her daughter in law for not bringing the scooter and television, so here they were accused of two sections such as 498 A , 304 B and was acquitted under 498 A. So in the case of the Queen Empress vs Huree Mohun Mythee, this husband has committed culpable Homicide under the criminal act. He has severely hurt her, which has led to the victim's death, and in this blood was oozing from the girl's body. The accused said it was due to sexual intercourse, which was false, and the court underwent a detailed investigation and said that this was not the case of Rape. Still, he was convicted for section 338 of 1PC and sentenced to one-year rigorous imprisonment.

In the case of Dowry death groom's family tend to take a defence by merely saying that their daughter in law has died due to kitchen accidents and fell from the staircase, and had health issues, Due to the demand for more dowry in the form of cash and equipment, the bride decide to kill herself [suicide] for the constant harassment and torture. And thus, prohibition has been made where they have brought the essentials for dowry death, in which the first condition is to have an injury or burn mark in her body. It should have been committed within seven years of marriage. They should be connected with the issue of dowry, and the instinct of torture or harassment should have taken place; lastly, this harassment and cruelty would have made her take extreme steps. So this essential is needed to be implemented when the dowry death case arises, which has been incorporated in section 304 B. The other form is bride burning. In this, they burn the daughter in law using the kerosene, and this all comes under the broad concept of Dowry death. It is also linked with sex-selective abortion, and if it is girl children, the parents tend to abort the fetus in the womb itself. So many states in our country have banned not informing the sex of the child. So various issues is connected where the demand for dowry will lead to the harassment and domestic violence can be some of the results of the dowry, So for the protection of women, section 498A which instil on the cruelty aspect to the bride and so the cruelty is not only by the husband and it also includes the family members of the bride groom's family and for this the punishment is for three years and fine or both. And third prevention is 113A Indian Evidence act, for demanding more dowry can be punished under this act. So the Judiciary, the body which delivers justice, makes the steps for solving the problem in the case of Kamlesh Paniyar vs State of Bihar, where the judge says that dream of the newlywed girl is shattered when she is harassed for dowry. He connects with terrorism and informs that terrorist is dowry. The protection is also there for failure to transfer of property where the punishment is imprisonment for six months to two years and fine up to 10000 and in case of the death of women the property should go, legal heir, if no children or parents for the women, they must give it to the trust.

Marriage in connection with the dowry death - Marriage is the institution that becomes the core base for dowry death and India. In this multi-religious country, marriage is interpreted as a sacrament according to Hindu beliefs. The dowry concept has been there for ages, and it has been approved and mentioned in the ancient texts in Manusmriti. So the dowry is given from the bride father to his son in law in the institution of marriage for taking care of his daughter. We can observe that women are always under the control of men. During her childhood, she is looked after by her father or brother and later after marriage, and she is under her husband's authority and later son. So, her entire life, she is being suppressed. The reason is the customs and daughter marriage is not so easy. It takes time, and dowry doesn't come in one settlement; the payment is always there till the marriage gets over. The dowry aspects through various elements are considered like education. The problem is due to the open-ended nature.

The dowry death has been increasing, even though the provisions have been made in section 5 mentions that receiving or giving dowry will be considered void. This offence is treated as cognisable and cannot make bail, and is non-compoundable. In contrast, the dowry death has been rising. The apparent reason is the domination of men over women, an intense feeling of gender inequality can be seen. In society, they treat women as a sexual object, and the next point is the customs are followed intensely. The way the Indian marriage is designed began from the Stridhan, the gift given from the bride's family; later, the gift has turned to dowry. After marriage, the new bride's dreams are shattered, and the circumstances make her take an extreme step like suicide or cause her to end her life by pushing her in stairs and making it look like an accident. The recent statistics by the National Crime Records Bureau [NCRB] has stated that seven thousand dowry cases have been registered in dowry deaths. Uttar Pradesh is the state which reports the highest number of dowry deaths. India is one of the countries which stands at the number one position in dowry in the world.

With the loopholes of the Dowry prohibition act 1961, the punishment for these heinous crimes was not severe. This act was a bit vague as it does not restrict the gifts which they get after the marriage and non-enforcement of the previous laws where the investigation is not serious done by the police officers. Merely they considered these cases as family disputes and registered them as accidents that have taken place in the kitchen. There is no proper implementation of the arrest of the guilty persons, where there are no proper photographs, and this leads the judge to decide and convict the guilty person. There is a chance where the groom's family has bribed police officer, and this will lead to delay in the court procedure, like filing the charge sheet and cultural attitude towards women were from girls childhood she has been taught to learn the basic skills like putting rangoli in front of their house and when she becomes matured, will be thought to learn cooking and then she will be made to do the household chores. When she comes to marriageable age, she will be asked to tolerate the family. These situations of the women can be seen in Phaniyamma by MK Indira and in the movie "The Great Indian Kitchen", where the crimes against women are portrayed. The next flaw is the economic discrimination against women. The paradox can be seen, where people who work for the stipulated time period is paid for their work and their salary is withdrawn. Still, women who manage to do all their household works. But she is neither paid, and if she is a working woman, she needs to balance both personal and professional life, but still, people tend to subjugate her in society. So they face discrimination against women, where they compare the salary between husband and wife. In the case of Sunil Balaji v State of Madhya Pradesh which points out the loopholes of section 304 B where the husband who demanded dowry amount after the marriage and then the girl used to ask her mother about the demand claimed by her husband, and she mentioned that her husband had illicit relationship with some girls. She could not tolerate it, and she committed suicide and then. The lower court verdict was not justifiable, and this was brought to appeal in the high court. It shows the negligence of the judiciary by not looking into section 304 B carefully. The judgment of the high court is considered as illegality. This dowry is practised in other Asian countries such as Pakistan, where they call it Jahez, Bangladesh and Iran, where this violence against women is carried, and also the main problem in many cases have been unreported, and women were not allowed to raise their voice in this matters.

India is one of the developing countries and it can be said that customs are given importance in our society, Crimes are happening everywhere, the victim suffers a lot and in that crime against women is observed in India, right from the girl child is born, the orthodox family become saddened and also take the decision of female infanticide, and then dowry and the situation of torture or cruelty of in-laws make her to take the extreme step, to end the life and then the society has created a taboo that women need to a dependant in their life. This highlights the effect of atrocities faced even when legal recognition and protection is guaranteed in the text but not in practice. So if we think in a rational manner, dowry death is murdering someone, and this evil social issue is considered not only illegal but also unethical in nature. This social stigma is against morality. Many provisions have been made in various states, such as the Dowry Prohibition act 1961. The dowry prohibition officers should be appointed to check and impose the punishment adhering to the crime committed and not convict.

In light of the existing laws, such as the dowry prohibition act of 1961, the necessary measures have been taken, yet the cases of dowry death in the country are rising to prohibit this social stigma. This should be nipped from the bud itself, which means we need to tackle the core cause for dowry death, So educating and creating awareness for girls, children and their families and make the society to think in rationale aspect, so as a whole we can curb this evil social issues impeding the development of the country. Laws should be made for the welfare of the people, so before passing, it must be discussed in the public platform and take the opinions and try to convince them for the progress of our country India. Literacy can make this situation better. If more people are educated, they will get a clear distinction between the customs and laws, making a shift towards an egalitarian society. Self-help groups and other schemes should be advanced in every part of the country, and good work always starts from home, so we need to share our domestic and they should be made that no discrimination must be made based on gender. The stricter laws must be included where the punishment must be made more rigid to get the fear.

<u>Author's Bio</u>

Madhumita.L, II year of B.A.,LL.B. from Christ University [School of Law] Bengaluru. I have taken up the social legal issue that is dowry death in India which is still prevailing in our society

CHAPTER SEVEN

IMPACT OF SINGAPORE CONVENTION IN THE INDIAN MEDIATION MARKET

Author: Amber Gupta, V year of B.A.,LL.B.(Hons.) from G.D. Goenka University, Gurugram, School of Law.

<u>Introduction</u>

Mediation has gained popularity and preference in India over the years, as the Indian legislature and courts have been inclined to establish the country's alternative dispute resolution system in line with international standards. This also stems from the fact that corporate organizations are increasingly preferring for strategies such as mediation over litigation. While mediation is widely used in India as a method of alternative conflict resolution when resolving family and civil law cases, various government bodies are taking aggressive steps to facilitate mediation as a means of dispute resolution.

Also, in 2015, the Indian Institute of Arbitration and Mediation signed an MOU with the Singapore International Mediation Centre to encourage the country's international trade mediation. After, in 2018, the Indian Parliament amended the 2015 Commercial Court Act and ordered the parties to have access to mediation before bringing a lawsuit before a Commercial Court. Nevertheless, following the affirmative actions, the development of international commercial mediation has been impeded due to some outbreaks. To demonstrate, a lack of sufficient laws and state mechanisms to implement a compromise agreement, inconsistency with interpretations of words such as conciliation and mediation, etc. Present a challenge in progressing the mediation method. The signing of the 2019 Singapore Mediation Convention comes as a positive change in the light of these concerns. This historic move is believed to cause an array of changes and developments regarding the growth of Indian commercial mediation.

The distinction between 'mediation' and 'conciliation'

The Convention, while describing the word 'mediation,' lacks the distinction between 'mediation' and 'conciliation' by its nomenclature. In the same way, some jurisdictions make interchangeably the use of the words "mediation" and "conciliation." The same does not hold for India, however, because there is ambiguity as to whether the two words are interchangeable. A simple reading of Section 89 of the Civil Procedure Code, 1908, and Section 30 of the 1996 Arbitration and Conciliation Act indicates that mediation and conciliation are defined as two distinct forms of conflict resolution. In comparison, India's Supreme Court has opined differently on many occasions. In the M/S Afcons Infra. Ltd. &Anr. vs Cherian VarkeyConstruction Co. (P) Ltd. &Ors. case, the Court claimed that mediation is synonymous with the word conciliation. A majority of leading voices on India's ADR system, such as Justice Indu Malhotra, also hold the same opinion. The use of the word 'conciliation' in the Act is proposed to include both mediation and conciliation, and if there is some discrepancy between the two procedures, the same is due to the facilitator's difference in the degree of involvement, which is not, in fact, a difference of practice.

The Convention has rectified this lack of clarity about the relationship between the two concepts, as it clearly describes the term mediation in Article 3 of its text. It clearly defines mediation as any mechanism that seeks to resolve conflicts by friendly resolution, supported by a third party, irrespective of the terms used to refer to that mechanism. This will serve as a roadmap to the enactment of the legislation in India and thus help to promote clarity about the reach of the two methods.

Another major hurdle affecting the country's development in international trade negotiations is the lack of awareness and practicability of international negotiations settlement agreements. Mediation under the aegis of the court is regulated by the Civil Procedure Code, and the settlement arrangement as a result of that mediation is implemented in the form of a court decree. Besides, a settlement arrangement forming part of an international arbitral award shall be implemented in compliance with Part II of Arbitration and Conciliation Act, 1996 as a consent award. Convention Article 1(3) precludes its application to mediations concluded either under the aegis of a trial or in arbitral proceedings in which the parties decide to use mediation rather than arbitration. These settlement arrangements may also continue to be followed as decrees of consent and awards of consent, respectively, and are beyond the scope of the Convention.

Also, settlement deals emerging from private negotiations are implemented as contracts in India. Thus, parties must initiate legal action to implement the terms of settlement as part of a verdict so that the settlement agreement achieves the sanction of law. The underlying flaw with this approach is that it requires the parties to obtain a decision in court after having sat through a lengthy mediation procedure, creating delay and frustration in the dispute resolution process. Besides, the legitimacy of such an arrangement may be questioned only based on Indian Contract Law's general principles and not based on the nature of the conflict.

Besides, the settlement agreements concluded by private conciliation are enforced by Part III of the Act. Under Section 73 of Arbitration and Conciliation act, 1996, where a conciliator defines 'elements of settlement' which are agreeable to the parties, a settlement arrangement may be chalked out after taking into account the parties' comments. This settlement agreement must be signed obligatory by the parties and certified by the conciliator to attach a binding effect to the settlement agreement.

Defined in section 74 of Arbitration and Conciliation Act, 1996, this Arrangement shall be considered to have the status and effect of an arbitral award on terms negotiated during arbitration proceedings. Although this legal fiction indeed protects the parties from the hassle of launching fresh compliance proceedings in court, at the same time it makes the settlement arrangement vulnerable to arbitral award challenges.

Because of the prevailing problems, the Convention's signing comes because of a respite as it provides for immediate acknowledgment and compliance of the settlement agreement, thus saving the parties from the difficulties of implementing the settlement agreements as arbitral awards or as decisions.

Accountability

The Parliament is required, according to Article 253 of the Indian Constitution, to enact legislation to give effect to any foreign Convention. India must, therefore, enact legislation that would govern the country's mediation mechanism. An important advantage of such promulgation is that it will assist in the establishment of a formal mediation system. India is also under an obligation to have sufficient state mechanisms in place to ensure the mediation process runs smoothly. Also, the government approved the establishment as a legislative body of the New Delhi International Arbitration Centre. There were reasons to establish such body in India, manage the ADR mechanisms adequately, Promoting ADR-sector research and development through workshops, conferences, training programs, etc, Create and manage a permanent Arbitrator's Panel and other administrative and support commissions for ADR facilities, Keep reports of government grants and all these were enacted under the New Delhi International arbitration centre act, 2019.

Conclusion

Expanding mediation as a means of resolving disputes will ease the burden on Indian courts that are infamous for being inundated with the backlog of cases. Besides this, the signing of the Convention has come as a strategic step on the part of India as it promotes foreign direct investment in the region. Foreign investors also concentrate on more convenient dispute resolution methods, such as mediation, rather than lengthy litigation. Being a party to the Convention warrants confidentiality, balanced results, cost reduction, and the preservation of business associations.

Author's Bio

This is Amber Gupta, fifth year student of a law school (B.A.LLB). Born and brought up in New Delhi. An optimistic, innovative, observant and motivated person who has got few aspirations alive that keep me moving ahead and teach me to never quit.

To cope with events and cases, the legal profession requires a great degree of hard effort and wit. I've always had an interest in this field. Those white shirts and pants with a white neck band and a black coat have always drawn my attention. Being a lawyer may appear to be an utopian dream for me, but it is much more than that. My skills, such as being able to articulate and clarify things, and questioning until my qualms fade, are well matched to my career. Regardless of the academic choice, we must always try to equip ourselves with insights and skills required to build a gratifying career. This understanding has always helped me in my academic performance and growth. Now that I have come to where my academic path is about to end and I have been trying to mold my professional skills, this aphorism has become even more relevant to me to grow even more skilled in my academic choice.

FARMERS RIGHT AND FOOD SECURITY LAWS IN INDIA: AN OVERVIEW

Author: Shalini Jha, II year of B.A.,LL.B. from School of Law, KIIT Deemed to be University, Bhubaneswar, Odisha, India

Co-author: Ananya Sinha, I year of B.B.A.,LL.B. from School of Law, KIIT Deemed to be University, Bhubaneswar,Odisha,India

<u>ABSTRACT</u>

In economic and livelihood activity farmers are the most active ones. They produce crops that include all agricultural commodities like poultries, fisheries, vermicomposting, sericulture, etc. Effective and improved knowledge of grains and reforms for agriculture has been shown in the Green Revolution. India has created agriculture policy success in wheat. Several acts and rights have been covered up for farmers' security. This paper aims to highlight farmers' rights and food security in India. The second section of this paper covers transitional practices of farming in modern India and challenges to food security. The government initiated a few steps to check up on farmers' security and remuneration. The third section of this paper covers the condition of farmers in the current situation. India's 1.3 billion populations are engaged in agriculture and they rely on it as their source of living, but the distressing fact is that agriculture contributes only 20% to India's GDP. Despite some stagnation, during the later modern era, the independent Republic of India was able to develop a comprehensive agricultural program.The year 2020 marked a significant change in the outlook of the government towards the problems which resulted in the passing of the agricultural acts which are popularly termed as 'Farm bills' which are used as a drive in the nation with people favoring them as well as with a section of people showcasing dissent towards the bills and it resulted in a nationwide protest. Food Security is a requisite for every country because of the various factors such as controlling the prices, economic growth and it provides a great boost to the agriculture sector. Food Security has been perturbed on several grounds in the recent past such as the climate change which as a whole affects the agriculture, overpopulation, corruption in the system at the lower levels which adds to the issue, lack of access to the resources are some of the factors behind the disruption in the food security in our country. This paper takes a subjective look at innovations and better approaches to agriculture practice. It also places the statistics on both the aspect of farmers' rights and bills as well as food security.[i]

KEYWORDS: agricultural economy, farmer's right, food security, farm bills, food mechanism

<u>INTRODUCTION</u>

"The simple hearth of the small farm is the true centre of our universe"
-Masanobu Fukuoka

The most vital aspect of the functioning of the country is the smooth generation and distribution of the food. It becomes even more essential to deliberate about the rights of the people who make the entire process so accessible for the country and the shape of the food security laws in our country. Farmer's rights and food security laws are the very pillar on which the operation of the food mechanism in our country stands. Farmers right refers to the rights which the farmers have to save, to use, exchange and to sell the produce and the seeds, it also includes the rights of the farmers to be appropriately recognized and honoured.They should be supported in all ways for their immense contribution to the global economy in terms of plant genetic resources and development of the various commercial varieties of the plants. It also expresses their rights to be included in the decision- making process which is related to the genetic resources of the crop.

According to the 'Protection of Plant Varieties and Farmer's Rights Act', 2001, it states that the specific right which is granted to the farmers which includes their Right of access to seeds which allows them to sow, save and sell their farm produce which also includes different varieties of seeds. Farmer's being the face of the entire agricultural economy of the country need a certain amount of protection and this comes in the form of rights which are entitled to them by the government.

<u>Farmer's rights</u>

1. **Right of sharing**: The benefit which states that the breeders and the legal entities which also includes the farmers who provide Plant Genetic Resources to the plant breeders for the purpose of developing the new varieties are entitled to receive the commercial gains from the vehicles which are registered.

2. **The Right to Compensation**: This act states that the seeds sold to the farmers, if they did not perform according to the expectations then they are entitled to claim compensation from the plant breeders.

3. **The Right to receive reward and considerable recognition**: Farmers should receive recognition for their contribution towards the conservation which provides them the necessary encouragement.

4. **The Right of protection of farmers from innocent infringement**: This is one right which gives them a chance to prove their innocence in front of the court. This right was enacted keeping in mind about the poor literacy rates of farmers.

5. **The Right of exemption**: This is regarding the registration fees related to the registration of the different plant varieties and also includes other services as well. The farmer's right in India is a subject of utmost deliberation as there are a number of farmers who are still not aware of their rights and are subjected to utmost cruelty at the hands of the big players in the food industry.

Food security in India

Food Security as stated by the United Nation Committee means that all the people, at all the times should have at least physical, economic and social access to hygienic, sufficient and nutritious food which in some ways meets the preferences of the people and which is necessary for an active and healthy life. Food Security is based on the three elements that are food accessibility, availability and utilization.

Historical aspect and evolution

Food Security in India has a tragic history, the Bengal Famine in the year 1949 which resulted in the loss of nearly 2 to 3 million lives due to starvation. The frequent droughts which happened during the colonial rule resulted in the loss of several lives. The nation has suffered several shocks in terms of food availability. Food Security is linked to various other factors of the economy including the prices of the food, agricultural growth and many other important mechanisms which forms the backbone of the economy.

Linkage of farmer's rights and food security

Farmers' Rights and the need for food security laws in India is a vis-à-vis issue which requires necessary deliberation as it forms a cornerstone of our food economy. The entire farm economy depends on these rights and laws which focus on the people who feed the entire country. Their contribution to the global food economy is immense and it becomes important that their rights are protected and their needs are attended to. Farmers' rights provide a valuable source of information regarding their difficulties. Protection of farmers' rights and taking initial steps for promotion should be the key objectives. Farmers' rights should be seen in a much broader perspective as a collective theme.

The basis of farmers' rights is a rich variety of medicinal plants, seeds, and trees. Genetic resources for agriculture are the basic customary rights of the farmers. Farmer's traditional knowledge of the correct usage of plant resources is farmers' free choice. The development of legislation can be meant for implementing and securing farmers' rights. Sustainable and conservative use of crop resources with greater financial support should go together with traditional knowledge of farmers about crops and food.

National food security act, 2013

The most recent food security act which aimed at figuring out the entire cause for the farmers was enacted i.e. The National Food Security Act, 2013 which brought a change in the entire concept of food security laws in India. The act turned around the concept of food security which was seen as a measure of welfare for the people to make it their right. The act entitled 75% and 50% of the rural and urban population to legally receive food grains at the subsidized rate under the targeted public distribution system. It gave certain rights to the women in order to empower them in the matters of the food security of their household. The enactment of the act showcased the necessity of the food security laws in India, not only at a domestic but on an individual level where it was kept in mind that every individual has access to healthy and nutritious food. The grim situation of not having access to food was to an extent started to change.[ii]

This Act was enacted by Manmohan Singh Indian National Congress which is led by the UPA government. This act was signed on 10 September 2013. Some of the programs of the national food security act are the mid-day meal scheme, the Public Distribution system, and integrated child development services. These schemes are 75% in the rural region and 50% of it in the urban region. Meeting the domestic demand as well as individual needs with adequate food quantities and prices is food security. Criticism of food security comes from both accusations of political motivation and fiscal irresponsibility.

The national food security bill has been highly contentious. Some of the features of this act are:-

1. **Households identification**- In the targeted Public Distribution System, the state identifies the households.

2. **Subsidized prices available**- food grains will be available at rupees 3/2 flash one per kg for rice-wheat and coarse grains for 3 years under Target Public Distribution. After that minimum support price will be linked to the subsidized prices.

3. **State coverage**- Central Government covers the state by using NSS household consumption survey data.

4. Entitlement and coverage under the Targeted Public Distribution System.

5. **Nutritional support and Maternity Benefit**- Rupees 6000 will be given to pregnant women and higher nutritional norms for up to 6-year-old malnourished children.

Traditional practices of farming in modern era

Farmers have their traditional practices of growing crops for food. Over the years despite modern equipment and technology, few methods of traditional farming are still being used.

1. **Agroforestry**-It is one of the oldest farming methods used to date. Multiple products and staple food crops can be grown from this method. This is useful in excess sunlight, wind, and controlling the temperature. This technique is useful in reducing soil erosion.

2. **Crop rotation**- Doctor Vandana Sharma founded this concept and this technique results in maximizing yields, minimizing the use of chemicals, and weed development.

3. **Intercropping /mixed crops**-Same land is used for cultivating mixed crops and is grown in multiple rows.

4. **Polyculture**-Faster sowing of seeds and better yield takes place by using this technique. Usage of chemicals and diseases can be controlled by this method.

5. **Water harvesting** -It is used for residential purposes and helps in the sustainable use of potable water. Water is stored either in a deep pit well or on rooftop houses.

Challenges to food security

1. **Overpopulation**- India is the second-most populous country in the world. As the consumption is more, production is to be relatively higher. Poverty is also a cause due to malnutrition.

2. **Migration**- People are migrating from the rural area to the urban areas in search of better health and hygiene and facilities which are lacking in slums and rural areas.

3. **Climate change**- Climate change causes trade disruption but also impacts livestock, farmers, and production output. Farming practices are difficult in high temperatures or high rainfall.

4. **Unmonitored schemes**- Proper implementation of Nutrition programs should be monitored.

5. **Irregular opening of ration shops**- Poor quality grains consumed by the buyers affect the health of the people.

6. **Lack of coordination**- Nutrition food with reaching out to poor people who can't afford to buy should be coordinated. Intersectoral coordination should be maintained between Ministries.

7. **Biofuel**- The biofuel market setup covers up a large area of land reducing the area for the growth of food crops.

<u>**Government initiatives to ensure food security**</u>

1. **Buffer stock**- government Procures stock of wheat and rice food corporation. Deficit areas and people who can't afford to get help from this.

2. **MSP (minimum support price) necessity**-A Pre announced price by the government for farmers' crops for raising production every year.

3. **Public distribution system**-This system was introduced in June 1997. The governments targeted and applied this principle in all areas.

4. **Cooperative role**- In Southern and western parts of the country shops are being set up within a cooperative society to set low prices.

<u>**Conditions of farmers**</u>

The condition of farmers in India has undergone changes in a very phased manner. The very backbone of the country i.e. the Indian agricultural economy has undergone dramatic metamorphosis for nearly seventy-five years from Independence. The country has been in a situation of not being reliant in terms of production of food to being a self-sufficient nation in the food sector. The farmers acted a key role in all these changing times but the condition of farmers in India has not undergone numerous changes. The condition of farmers in India has not seen a significant change; we still have to hear about farmer suicides because they are not able to pay off their loans. The situation of low income received by the farmers still exists, all these are some of the reasons which depicts the indigent picture of the complexities which the farmers have to face on a daily basis.

These difficulties have been existing since ages and the schemes and plans of the government have not been efficient in discovering a long term solution to these problems which are looming on the agricultural productivity of the nation. These also act as a burden for the farmers of the country. The grim situation of the agricultural economy can be perceived from the condition of farmers in India.

The farmer suicide in India which is always at a rise because of the inability of the farmers to repay their loans is one of the several reasons which reflect the disheartening situation of the farmers. There has been conflicting reasons for these deaths, claims have addressed the anti-farmer laws, failure to pay the debt, unexpected failure of the crop growth and various mental health issues as the reason behind the extremely high farmer suicide rate figures in India.

The decreasing area of the land allocated for agricultural purposes adds to the misery as the land-holdings of the farmers decrease which reduces the farm produce. The small land-holdings force the farmers to sell off their produce locally and they are not able to get fair prices for their produce.

According to the report released by the Situation Assessment of Agricultural Households and Land and Holdings of Households in Rural India, 2019 reveals the distressing data about the low income of the farmers, and the average monthly income which is received by them from different other sources of per agricultural household in July 2018 and 2019 brings out to be only Rs. 10,218 which computed according to paid-out approach states that the per day income of the household of the farm is just Rs. 277 which is not much from what is received by the farmers from the employment scheme.

The three farm bills which were Farmer's Produce Trade and Commerce (Promotion and Facilitation) Act, 2020, Farmer's (Empowerment and Protection) Agreement of Price Assurance and Farm Services Act, 2020 and Essential Commodities (Amendment) Act, 2020. The Farmer's Produce Trade and Commerce (Promotion and Facilitation) Act,2020 aimed at giving the farmers an opportunity to get themselves engaged in the trade of their produce outside the physical markets which is mentioned under the various state Agricultural Produce Marketing Committee Acts. This act would have overruled these state acts and aimed to promote hassle-free inter and intra state trade. The act also proposed an e-platform for trading of the produce directly. The organizations which can engage in this trading could be partnership firms, societies and companies. The main rationale behind the act was to allow the farmers to trade outside these state designated APMC and prohibit the state government from levying any taxes. The Farmers (Empowerment and Protection) Agreement of Price Assurance and Farm Services Act, 2020 focused on providing the farmers with a proper framework which will serve as a guide for them to enter into contract farming, giving them an opportunity to enter into agreement with the buyer on the onset of the sowing season and they have a chance to sell off their produce pre-determined prices. The act allows entering into contract with entities known as 'sponsors', who can enter into contract and agree on mutual issues such as fodder, seed etc.

The agreements are valid for one cropping season and prices for the produce is also added as an important clause in the agreement. The most important part of the act which was an issue of contention and to a certain extent a reason for nationwide protest was the absence of the Minimum Support Price which was mentioned in the act. The act also provided the three level dispute settlement mechanisms. The Essential Commodities (Amendment) Act,2020 aimed at restricting the authority of the government with respect to certain key factors of agriculture related to production, supply and the distribution of the produce.

The act removed certain important products like pulses, cereals etc. from the essential commodity list. The government set up stock limits for the produce according to the market price. The price was determined according to the rise in the market price. It somewhat removed the involvement of the private players in the market and gave freehand to the three essential components of agriculture i.e. production, supply and distribution.

The acts were met with severe criticism across the nation which eventually led to it being repealed by the central government. The criticism was on the basis of several provisions of the act which includes the uneasiness among the farmers in northern states of Punjab and Haryana was about the deconstructing of Minimum Support Prices (MSP), the farmers feared about the big corporate dictating the prices and the fear of the farmers of getting loss for their agricultural produce. The proposal to regulate the trade given by the central government was not well received by the farmers and their issue of contention was that the laws had no provision for regulating the traders in the business. The contract farming clause which allowed the farmers to approach the courts in case as promised that their land will not be used for the purpose of giving loans and mortgaging of the lands as mentioned in the acts.

The proposal was not meant with great appreciation as the farmers' claim against this provision of the act was the long standing history related to contract farming which has resulted in the occupying of the lands of the farmers due to non-payment of dues.

Farmer suicides and in-dept issues have remained unresolved for decades in India. The standing committee on Agriculture found out that the Farm acts were not being implemented by Indian Agriculture markets or working honestly.

Farmer bills, 2020

In June 2020, three acts were promulgated:-

1. Farmers produce trade and commerce (promotion and facilitation) act, 2020-Electronic trading and e-commerce are to be practiced. Expanding selected areas for farming. Levying of market fee or on farmers, cess, and the electronic platforms by the State governments is strictly prohibited.

2. Farmers (empowerment and protection) agreement on price assurance and the farm services act, 2020-This act provides a legal framework and dispute resolution mechanism. Farmers can enter into pre-arranged contracts with the buyers.

3. Essential Commodities (Amendment) Act, 2020- This act removes stockholding limits on agriculture items such as cereals, onions, edible oils, and many more from the list of essential commodities produced by horticulture. These three farm laws were tabled in Punjab, Rajasthan, and Chattisgarh to amend.

A piece of complete information is provided by these Farm acts. Farmer's response was a bit supportive in Maharashtra. They believed in the bills and wanted to decide the price of agricultural commodities. The opposition reason was the uncertainty in the implementation of the farm acts. Low bargaining power and minimum support price was also the center point for opposition to the bills. The three acts were repealed on 1st December 2021.

Steps ensuring better approaches for agriculture practices

India ranks 71 out of 113 countries according to the food security index 2020. The Food Corporation of India has played a vital role in India Karnataka Andhra Pradesh Tamil Nadu up and Chhattisgarh forwarded schemes providing good nutrition to the people.

" Indira canteen" which is launched by Karnataka serves three times the food a day and is very affordable. Tamilnadu initiated' AmmaVnavagam' which was proposed by the Nimbkar agricultural research Institute.

The State of UP passed a food bill ensuring not to throw away leftover food from the parties rather than to distribute it to needy people 2013. Chhattisgarh government enacted Food Security Act ensuring nutrition food at a low price to everyone in the state. 138 crore people of India is a challenge for food production. It is hard to meet every individual's needs in the country and ensure access to food for them. Per unit of land and irrigation water is needed for agriculture. Financial problems become a hurdle for the families who can't afford to buy food and this is the reason many children around India are malnourished.The protein-rich diet should be more available and affordable. Environmental friendly Technology should be used with minimum land and water. Biogas can be used as a surplus with mined natural gas for the production of poultry, fish, and protein-rich cattle.

Stability of price economic balance with the price rise should be maintained. Supply of goods will supply money wholesale price the price of all would be the wholesale price index of the Indian economy. Fiscal measures, monetary measures, administered price mechanisms and the Public Distribution system are certain steps to control price rise.

India's fertilizer subsidy burden can be reduced by shifting to green ammonia. It can reduce the dependence on imports of Expensive Liquefied Natural Gas (LPG) for fertilizer manufacturing. This can boost self-reliance energy too. Fertilizer demand is expected to go over the years and the need for liquefied natural gas imports.We should keep to the more domestically produced feedstock and a cleaner environment. Grey hydrogen is produced from natural gas or methane which acts as a feedstock for Ammonia production; this can be replaced by Green hydrogen which is produced by electrolysis of water which is powered by renewable energy. Green Ammonia can be produced by using various other electricity inputs such as the grid electricity.

CONCLUSION

The laws established with a view of improving the conditions of the farmers have not been perceived well with the ultimate beneficiary of them as was in the case of farm bills but the government is working rigorously towards framing laws which will improve the conditions of the farmers. The future ahead to this is that the government with due deliberation and negotiation with the stakeholders make laws which can solve the problems of the farmers. This is the only way we can resolve the numerous issues surrounding them.[iii]

The issues of employment, low income, are quite substantial matters affecting the lives and families of several farmers across the nation. The need of the hour is to look beyond the loopholes and corruption of the system and find a way to deal with these problems. The conditions of the farmers can be improved if the government with their constant efforts continues to work for the benefit of the farmers.

PROTECTION OF CHILDREN FROM SEXUAL OFFENCE, ACT 2012

Author: Giftlin Melba J, IV year of B.A.,LL.B. from

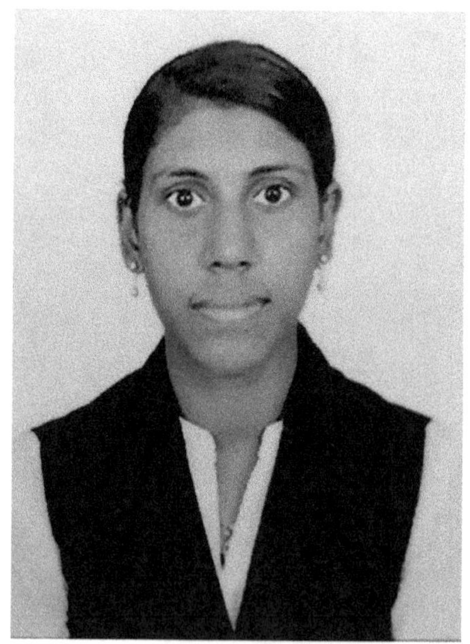

Introduction

The Protection of Children from Sexual Offences Act is a comprehensive act that came into force in November 2012. The Act has been enacted to protect children from offences of sexual assault, sexual harassment and pornography and provide for establishment of Special Courts for trial of such offences and related matters and incidents. It covers all types of sexual abuse

Features of the Act

1. This act defines varioustypes of offencessuch as pornographic crimes,touch based,non-touched based all in a detailed form

2. If a child faces any abuse in their home that child will be taken to child welfare commission for a good care and protection

3. Here there is no gender difference unlike rape in ipc where only the female is always considered as the victim

4. During the investigation process a policeman is appointed to the child so that it will not be re-victimized 5. Section 45 of this act explains that the rules for this act can be taken by the central government

6. Section 42 A of the act explains that if the judgment cannotbe made becauseof the interference of the other laws, then the pocso act can override them

7. For the statement recordingthe police officermust move to place where he/she is convenient and with the person who they trust

8. Female doctors only will be allowed for the forensic evidence to be collected from the child with the person of trust

9. Once if the testimony of the child is given in a video link then he/she will not be compelled again to repeat it in the court

10. It also prescribes punishment to the people who traffic children for sexual purposes.

Implementation of pocso act

The Pocso act came into force on November 14,2012. It is specifically formed to reduce the child sexual abuseand the childpornoghraphics. The Pocso Act 2012 explains the recording way from the children by thepoliceman in a friendly manner. This act includes46 provisions.

Punishments under the act

1. Penatrative sexual assault caused for the child is punishable upto not less than 7 years of imprisonment it can be extended to life imprisonment also. But the pocso amendment bill passed in the year 2012 extended the punishment from 7 years to 10 years.

2. Sexual assault committed on a child below 16 years will be punished with not less than 20 years of imprisonment in some cases it may extend to death penalty also.

3. If a child is used for a pornography purpose he/she will be punished by imprisonment from 7years to 9 years. But the amendment in the year 2019 reduces it minimum 5 years and maximum 7 years

4. Any person commits assault under trust or authority then he/she will be punished with imprisonment of 5 years to 7 years and fine under section 10.

5. If a policeman failedto report an offense in the child welfare committeethen he will be punished with 6 months imprisonment and/or fine under section 21.

General principles of pocso act

The child must be protected from all sorts of physical and mental abuse. Harmonious development of a child is very important in society. In the justice process the child victims must be treated well.The process of justice will be transparent, irrespective of the child's culture,and the religiousare to be punished.The victimized child should not be re-victimized so they will be given protection and they will be taught self-defense.

All the proceedings that are to be done will be informed to the child beforehand.The act was amended in 2019. person can be charged with this offence in certain aggravating circumstances, such as if the rape occurs within a relationship of trust or authority, or if it leads to pregnancy, among. This act was mainly enactedto stop the cruelty that takes part in the life of the child in their day to day life.

Observation of pocso Act

The Pocso Act mustbe avalued act among the country. The act plays a role in taking our nation forward,it is a duty of every citizen of our country to know this act. Sexual cruelty is the nationalissue in our country,most of the statessuffer with it,sexual includes the touches and non-touches. Not only this but pornography crime is the major issue now a days. Threatening people with pornographic must be strictly prohibited. Many laws had been created but the sexual harassment cannot be controlled till date. Lots of porn sites are still in progress,so this must be strictly prohibited and the publishers also must be punished. Otherwise this encourages many to harass people.

Case laws

Delhi Nirbhaya case

In the year 2012 on December 16 in delhi a girl was gang raped in the bus. A 22 year old physiotherapy intern was beaten,gang raped and tortured in the bus in which she was traveling.6 members raped her including the driver. The 6 convictswere arrested, 1 had died in the police custody, 4 were given death sentence, and 1 was under the age of 18 so he was imprisoned for 3 years under the juvenile justice law.

Jarnail singh v. State of Haryana

In the year of 2013 a savitri devi's daughter was raped when she was at sleep. But the convict who committed it was under the age of 18 so he has been punished under the juvenile justice and handed him in the care and protection center of the government.

CHAPTER TEN

LENIENCY REGIME IN INDIA

Author: Esha Sharma, II year of B.Com.,LL.B.(Hons.) from Nirma University

Introduction A leniency programme is a type of whistleblower protection, i.e., an official system of providing leniency to a cartel member who reports the cartel to the Commission. In exchange for immunity or lenient treatment, competition authorities have devised a variety of leniency programmes to encourage and incentivize various actors involved in the commission of such competition infringements to come forward and disclose such anticompetitive agreements and assist the competition authorities. The leniency programme protects those who come forward and submit information honestly, who would otherwise face harsh action from the Commission if the existence of a cartel is discovered on its own. To better understand the leniency programme, we must look at what are cartels. Cartels are basically groups of manufacturers or sellers who come together to maximize their profits through price fixing, limiting supply, or other means. These types of agreements and associations discourage healthy market competition, thereby impeding the survival and growth of market competitors. The advantage of using leniency programmes to expose cartels, which is quite scheming is further encouraged by antitrust regimes all over the world for the favorable implementation of competition law and policies. The formation of a cartel is a heinous offence under the Competition Act 2002. Section 46 of the Competition Act and the Competition Commission of India (Lesser Penalty) Regulations 2009 govern the Indian leniency regime (Leniency Regulations). The Competition Commission has the authority to investigate any cartel and impose a penalty of up to three times its profit for each year of the agreement's continuation, or ten percent of its turnover for each year of the agreement's continuation, whichever is greater. In exchange for immunity or lenient treatment, competition authorities have devised a variety of leniency programmes to encourage and incentivize various actors involved in the commission of such competition infringements to come forward and disclose such anti-competitive agreements and assist the competition authorities. The CCI has the authority to grant complete immunity or a reduction in penalties to a whistleblower who makes a "full, true, and vital disclosure" about the cartel's alleged offences, provided that the leniency applicant meets certain criteria: 1. completely stops participation in a cartel (unless directed otherwise by the CCI). 2. does not hide, eliminate, manipulate or dislodge any material information that is important. 3. proceeds to comply with the CCI honestly, entirely, constantly and expeditiously until the proceedings are completed. 4. and conforms with any other limitation or regulations imposed by the CCI. The CCI offers a penalty reduction based on a marker system. The first leniency applicant would be given the first 'priority status' under the marking system if they either: 1. give evidence that allows the CCI to develop a prima facie opinion on the cartel (i.e., submit material to the CCI to launch an investigation by the Office of the Director General (DG));

2. or supply evidence that allows the CCI to establish the cartel's formation. Following then, if successive leniency applicants submit relevant material that adds considerable value to the evidence already available with the CCI, they will be given penalty reductions. As a result, all leniency applicants (beyond first priority status) would be required to produce evidence that would aid the CCI or DG in establishing the infringement. If the leniency applicant receives second priority status, he or she may be given a penalty reduction of up to or equal to 50% of the entire penalty levied. Penalty reductions of up to or equal to 30% of the total penalty levied will be awarded to leniency applicants with the third or subsequent priority category. In India's leniency system, there were just three markers accessible till 2017. Background The first ever leniency application was filed in response to the CCI's Suo moto investigation into cartelization in Indian Railways tenders by manufacturers of brushless DC fans. Despite the fact that the investigation for this case began with information provided by the Central Bureau of Investigation, one of the parties, M/s Pyramid Electricals, filed a leniency application during the investigation. M/s Pyramid Electronic was the first and only party to disclose key facts in this matter, including the existence of a bid-rigging cartel, according to the CCI. The evidence received by CCI backed up Pyramid's claims. Given that the

applicant provided comprehensive collaboration, CCI viewed such cooperation in connection with, rather than in isolation from, the value of the disclosed information. In other words, because Pyramid addressed the CCI after the investigation had commenced, the CCI did not offer a complete reduction in penalty. Initially, the leniency regime was limited to 'enterprises' (i.e., an entity having economic operations). Despite this, the CCI granted leniency to an individual who volunteered information on the bid-rigging of tenders issued by Indian Railways for the supply of fans in its first leniency decision on 18 January 2017. Issues The efficiency of the leniency regime, or rather its lack thereof, may be shown in the fact that only ten leniency orders have been issued in the ten years after the Regulations were enacted. The reason for this, it could be argued, is the CCI's enormous discretionary powers. The CCI may grant lighter penalties to an applicant who ceases to be a cartel member, according to the Regulations. Applicants must, however, reveal all relevant papers, continue to cooperate, and adhere to any conditions imposed by CCI in exchange for immunity or a reduced penalty. This adds a layer of ambiguity, which deters enterprises involved in cartelization from coming out and providing information. Furthermore, immunity and lighter fines can be revoked under the Indian framework if the CCI determines that the circumstances on which such leniency was granted were not met, the petitioners provided misleading evidence, or the information made was not necessary. Need for Proper Marker System in India When a cartel has more than one member, it is possible that applications from cartel members who have formed a single cartel will be received at the same time. This causes a lot of uncertainty about the queue's order. This order is extremely important since it determines whether or not a fine or penalty will be reduced. There is a lack of openness, and concerns may be raised about who was kept ahead of whom in the cartel. As a result, a marking system was developed to reserve and safeguard a cartel member's spot in a leniency queue for a specific period of time. One of the reasons for the leniency program's poor performance in India is the lack of a well-defined marker system. Although Indian law stipulates that an applicant shall be 'marked' after filing an application with the Commission either in writing (including e-mails, faxes, and the like) or orally. However, because to the lack of a concrete marker mechanism, a leniency application will only be allowed a marker if he or she provides vital information in order to make a landmark change or initiate actions against the cartel. Lessons can be learned from the European Union's marker system, which was implemented in 2006. A marker system can also be beneficial for gathering further information about new cartels that may emerge at a later date. As a result, detecting cartels on a long-term basis may be advantageous. It is necessary to develop a marker system. The marker system, as seen in the EU and the US, has played a significant influence in the improvement of leniency policies. In addition, an appropriate level of transparency and disclosure must be maintained. Confidentiality Clause in the System Another significant concern is that whistleblowers must be assured of maintaining confidentiality and secrecy after providing firsthand knowledge. The fact that the first leniency application, Phoenix Conveyer Belt, India, has come forward and revealed the creation of a cartel in the conveyor belt industry indicates that the CCI has failed to offer the appropriate level of confidentiality to such leniency applicants. The applicant's identity should ideally be kept hidden until anything tangible has been established. In this sense, it is possible to argue that a physical marker system can assist in keeping such concealment even if further petitions for such leniency are made. This is due to the fact that the applicant just receives a marker and has no knowledge of the marker holders who came before or after him. He is just conscious of his place in the line. However, in the absence of a legitimate, transparent structure, it is difficult to empower people to do so. In addition, the legislation includes the phrase "vital disclosure" as a requirement. However, amnesty does not define what constitutes such crucial information. The Act's definition renders the provision generic, allowing the CCI to apply it to any situation. They are free to interpret as they see fit. Furthermore, the initial cartel member's disclosure of information receives complete immunity. Surprisingly, the second candidate to reveal details, Validating the existence of such a cartel does not entitle you to 100% immunity or a reduction in your sentence. Under the definition of 'added value,' he will be entitled to a decrease. The phrase "vital information" used in Regulation 4 of the Lesser Penalty Regulation needs to be defined in order to clear up any misunderstanding.

The leniency programme is a good and proper alternative made by the Commission in order to combat market cartelization, which disrupts market equilibrium. It's also vital to remember that a leniency programme won't work until the cartels are penalized. If there are no strict restrictions in place, such programmes will be considered a failure. The Commission's role is critical in every phase of the programme, from the moment the application for these arrangements is received until the proceedings are concluded. The Commission should consider the application seriously and respond appropriately within the time range provided. It should ensure that the highest level of secrecy is maintained. The commission should also evaluate and review whether the applicant's information is relevant, vital, or not in relation to the application. It should work with the applicant at every level of the process and conduct the inquiry in a timely manner. The Commission also has the responsibility to ensure that the applicant cooperates with them as much as possible throughout the investigation, and that only the leniency provisions are applied to the applicant's case. If the applicant fails to do so, the commission must ensure that he is held accountable and tried under the penalty provisions if he did not make the disclosures. The Commission also has the responsibility to monitor and investigate the market for new methods and ideas that should be incorporated into the leniency provisions in order to compel individuals or businesses to come forward and disclose relevant information about arrangements that harm the market's equilibrium.

Author's Bio

My name is Esha Sharma. I am a second-year law student, currently pursuing B.Com LLB (HONS) from

Institute of Law, Nirma University.

CHAPTER ELEVEN

VIOLENCE AGAINST WOMEN IN INDIA

Author: Suchita Garg, I year of LL.M. from Sabarmati University

<u>Abstract</u>

Women and girls in South Asia are born into a societal and traditional system steeped in inequity and discrimination. They are given an unfair share of opportunities, attention and resources from the instant of their formation. One of the most challenging and threatening signs of gender based inequity is violence against women and girls.

It is being gradually recognised by policy makers in India that violence against women and girls is a serious restraint to the success of the country's development goals. This fear has prompted legal reforms, new legislation, beefing up of institutional mechanisms for the advancement of women and instituting policies that seek to address women's vulnerability in various regions.

Violence against women and girls is embedded in unequal power relations between men and women in society and can be well understood within a gender framework. While sex is a biological category, gender is a social construct and refers to widely shared expectations and norms within society about appropriate male and female behaviour, characteristics and roles.

In South Asia, violence against women and girls has been viewed along a continuum of incremental discrimination that renders them vulnerable to violations in several spheres of their lives. Gender based inequality exists in all stages of women's lives- from infancy to old age and manifests in the form of several acts of violence.

Introduction

Violence within the family is widespread and affects women throughout the society in wealthy urban households as much as in the poorest rural households, across all the religious, class and caste boundaries. Domestic violence refers to any act of violence in the house- it includes differential treatment of girls, wife beating and abuse, torture of daughters-in-laws and lack of care of widowed women in the family. The perpetrators are close relatives of the woman-father, husband and his family, sometimes even the son. Domestic violence is part of abusive behaviour and control rather than an isolated act of physical anger. Physical violence in intimate relationship is practically always accompanied by psychological abuse and, in one- third to over one-half of cases, by sexual abuse.

Violence within marriage in India is often linked with the practice of dowry although it is by no means the only cause of violence. Dowry demands can increase into harassment, threats, and abuse; in extreme cases the woman is killed or driven to suicide, releasing the husband to pursue another marriage and dowry.

Domestic violence is also denoted to as a 'silent crime' because of woman's inability to speak about the violence inflicted on them due to shame, fear of further abuse on themselves or their children and lack of options. Thus domestic violence is frequently ignored, underestimated or denied by the family, judicial system (police, prosecutors and by judges), public and women(victims).

In South Asia, India has some of the most extensive acts and a large legal machinery to protect the rights of women. The government of India (GOI) has adopted a number of approaches to address countless dimensions of violence against women. There has been a clear shift from viewing women as beneficiaries of improvement, to equal partners in the development process. The government has been forthcoming in implementing legal reforms and designing programmes aimed at the empowerment of women. However, the implementation of the same is embedded in notions of the family.

Laws related to domestic violence

Domestic violence as a criminal act was known only in 1986 in India after strong advocacy by the women's movement. The laws that deal with domestic violence are:

- Section 498A of the Indian Penal Code addresses physical and mental cruelty committed by the husband and his relatives. It is a cognisable, non- bailable offence and has been lauded for its deterrent effect. Cruelty is defined to include any conduct that drives married women to commit suicide or cause grave danger or injury to her life, limb of health, whether mental or physical. It is also includes harassment of the women to coerce her or her relatives to meet unlawful demands for property or other valuables.
- Section 304B, IPC (1961) was introduced in order to strictly deal with and punish the offence of dowry harassment and death.
- The Dowry Prohibition Act was amended in 1984 and later in 1986, whereby any property, article, gifts etc. given by the girl parents before, at the time, or after marriage was defined as dowry. The punishment for dowry was increased and it was made a cognisable and non- bailable offence. The burden of proof shifted on the accused and made police investigation obligatory with respect to the unnatural death of women.
- Section 174 of the Criminal Procedure Code was revised by the Criminal Law Act, 1983 to provide for investigation by the police of cases of suicide committed by women or death of women taking place in suspicious circumstances within 7 years of marriage.
- Section 113 and 133B were inserted in the Indian Evidence Act,1872 these provisions lay down that if a woman who commits suicide within

7 years of her marriage due to 'Cruelty' by her husband or his relatives, the court may presume that suicide had been abetted by her husband or by his relatives.

Sexual Violence

Sexual violence is a violence of the basic human right "to live with dignity and without fear" there are many forms of violence: eve teasing, molestation, rape- within or outside marriage, child sexual abuse and sexual harassment in the work place. Sexual violence against women and young girls can happen anywhere- on the streets, at home, in public or private places- by strangers or by members of the family. Sexual violence, either a one- time assault or protracted abuse, damages concepts of sexual intimacy, trust and a sense of the overall well-being of women.

Sexual assault includes all forms of non-consensual contact with a sexual purpose ranging from eve teasing to molestation to rape. It also include touching or fondling and all forms of penetration. The study also indicates that most sexual assaults cases occur at home and the largest percentage of these occur at the victim's home during the daytime. A study of judgments by the Supreme and High courts on rape cases in India Between 1950-1990 revealed that 54% of the rape cases researched took place between 6 AM and 7 PM.

Marital rape, though not widely accepted as crime by communities and law in India, is also experienced by a number of women within the four walls of the home.

Another common form of sexual violence against woman is Sexual Harassment in the Workplace. In the words of the Supreme Court of India, sexual harassment constitutes a serious violation of women's fundamental rights to freedom and equality at the workplace. In 1997, the SC issued guidelines against sexual harassment for both the public and the private sector. Sexual harassment, as defined by the Supreme Court order, is any unwelcome physical contact and advances, demand or request for sexual favours, sexually coloured remarks, display of pornography and any other kind ofunwelcome physical, verbal or non-verbal conduct of a sexual nature.

Child sexual abuse, like other forms of violence against women, can happen to any child, anywhere often through adults known to the child. It is a common phenomenon. Child Sexual Abuse refers to any sexual act that occurs between an adult or an immediate family member and a child, and any non-consensual sexual contact between a child and a peer.

Conclusion

In India, violence against women is still seen at the individual level. The fact that Indian women are dependent on men at all levels and not only/necessarily financially makes them especially vulnerable to violence whether domestic or sexual. However the general tendency, particularly by the police and the judiciary is to treat such cases on their individual merit rather than emphasize this power imbalance. This would require not just legislative changes but changing the ground reality where women are actually empowered and not endowed with mere paper rights.

In India, the legal provisions have been tentative. At the point of initiation, they inevitably contain some wide loopholes which allow men to escape scot-free and between the accused/offender and the victim/prosecutrix make it more difficult for the latter to prove her case. Ironically, as and whenever the violence suffered by women reaches serious proportions, and more importantly , leads to public outrage, the state typically responds by modifying the existing penal provisions and adding more stringent provisions. The 'stringent provisions ' often remain on paper with a marked reluctance shown by the police to register cases and the judiciary giving the tacit impression that women are misusing the laws made for their protection. The legal codes have not been effective in protecting women. Nor has it succeeded in ensuring justice for the victims by way of retribution. Whether it is at birth, during lifetime or eventual death, the laws appear to be strong enough to act as deterrents but reality speaks a different story.

The Indian state formulates some principles to deal with gender-violence, takes scant interest in implementing them, thereby allowing rate of violence to grow. When such violence grows out of proportion, making the people seethe in anger it spells danger for the state. Then the governmental machinery responds typically with setting up of specialist agencies and framing new and 'stricter laws' which continue to remain on paper.

Author's Bio

Suchita Garg is a student in Sabarmati University. She is pursing LLM degree in Criminal and Security laws. She worked hard as an intern at various courts of India. She likes to write about the current happenings around her. The author wrote on this topic because she wants that readers should understand that violence against women is a crime which we see around us but fails to raise our voice. She also wants to draw the attention of the readers towards the condition of women in different religions and places in India.

CONNECTING FUNDAMENTAL RIGHTS TO HUMAN RIGHTS: A STUDY ON ARTICLE 21 OF INDIAN CONSTITUTION

Author: Mr. Debarghya Bhattacharya, Assistant Professor from Kristu Jayanti College of Law, Bengaluru.

Co-Author: Ms. Astha Sen, 1st year, BBA., LL.B. from Kristu Jayanti College of Law, Bengaluru.

INTRODUCTION

Fundamental Rights are the basic rights of the human beings. Everyone has the authority to utilize these rights. India is a country of freedom, secularism, and sovereignty where each and every individual gets equal rights. These rights are written in the Indian Constitution under Part III. Fundamental Rights cover right to life, freedom of speech, freedom of religion, liberty of thoughts etc.

The outline of Fundamental Rights:

Since the 17th century, the idea that man has certain fundamental, natural, and inalienable rights or freedoms, has permeated into human thought. According to this theory, the state's role is to recognise these rights and freedoms and grant them freedom of expression in order to preserve human liberty, foster the development of the human personality, and advance an effective social and democratic life.

Human rights have their roots in the natural law thinkers like Locke and Rousseau. Philosophers who studied natural law pondered these inalienable human rights and proposed the social compact idea in an effort to uphold them.

"Man is born with the title to absolute freedom and the unrestricted enjoyment of all the rights and privileges of the law of nature," said Locke, "and he has by nature a power to safeguard his property, namely his life, liberty, and estate, against the insults and attempts of other men". The French Revolutionary Declaration of 1789, which was influenced by Lockeian theory and can be seen as a specific political statement on human rights, said that "the purpose of all political union is the conservation of the natural and inalienable rights of man".

The European Convention on Human Rights and the United Nations Organization's charter of human rights have given the idea of people's fundamental rights, a more tangible and universal texture in modern times. The Preamble to the Universal Declaration of Human Rights, among other things, stated that, "Whereas acknowledgment of the inherent dignity and of the equal and inalienable rights of all members of the human family is the foundation of freedom, justice, and peace of the world".

Thus, the idea of fundamental rights denotes a trend in contemporary democratic thought. Modern constitutional law places a lot of emphasis on the protection of human rights. The idea of natural law and natural rights is the source of the inclusion of fundamental rights as unforeseen rights in contemporary constitutional papers and the widely accepted Charter of Human Rights.

The idea of connecting India's fundamental rights to global human rights has been increasingly popular in recent years. The Supreme Court of India has referenced the International Declaration on Human Rights when interpreting the Articles of the Indian Constitution pertaining to fundamental rights. For instance, the Supreme Court frequently cites the 1948 Universal Declaration of Human Rights, noting that "the applicability of the Universal Declaration of Human Rights and principles thereof may have to be read, if necessary, into the domestic law".

Fundamental Rights vis-a-vis Human Rights

As the name implies, fundamental rights are the fundamental freedoms that all people of a nation are entitled to and that have been upheld by the Supreme Court and accepted by the general public. These are characterised as basic rights because they are protected by the constitution and are upholdable in a court of law. As a result, they are referred to as such because an individual may go to court to have his or her rights upheld in the event that they are violated. No one is exempt from the application of fundamental rights, regardless of caste, religion, gender, race, or place of origin. It protects civil liberties so that each and every citizen of the nation can live their life as they like.

Human rights are universal, absolute, and fundamental moral demands in that they belong to all people, are inalienable, and are required for a real life. These are essential for everyone, regardless of caste, creed, nation, place of birth, citizenship, or any other status. The same human rights apply to everyone, without exception. These rights are basic rights held by those who support justice, equality, freedom, and respect for all. These are crucial for the advancement of society since they do away with wrongdoing, exploitation, prejudice, and inequality, among other behaviours. The freedom from discrimination, the right to life, equality before the law, liberty and personal security, the right to education, the freedom of thought, the right to free movement, etc. are some examples of common human rights.

Article 21 of Indian Constitution, 1950: An umbrella provision

Human rights were grossly violated by the ruling class in India under British rule. As a result, the framers of Indian Constitution, many of whom had spent a lengthy time behind bars under the British system, had a highly positive view of these rights.

Everyone agreed on the necessity of having fundamental rights, and as a result, the Constituent Assembly did not even discuss whether or not to include such rights in the constitution. The fight has actually always been against the limitations placed on them, and the goal has always been to get the fundamental rights applied to as many people as possible.

Part III of the Constitution protects substantive as well as procedural rights. The chapter's inclusion in the Constitution follows the currents of contemporary democratic philosophy. The goal is to protect some fundamental rights from the vicissitudes of politics. Fundamental rights have two functions: first, they restrain the complete power of the legislature, and second, they create the framework for the greater development of our people, including the preservation of their inherent dignity.

According to Article 21, no one may be deprived of their life or personal freedom unless doing so in accordance with a legal process. The words "process established by law" are crucial in this clause.

Immediately after the constitution became effective the question of interpretation of these words arose in the famous Gopalan Case and where the validity of the Preventive Detention Act, 1950 was challenged. The main question was whether Article 21 envisaged any procedure laid down by a law enacted by the legislature or whether the procedure should be fair and reasonable.

By a majority decision, the Supreme Court held that the word "law" in Article 21 could not be interpreted to mean the principles of natural justice. These regulations were imprecise and ambiguous, and the constitution could not be interpreted as establishing a hazy standard. The term "law" was never employed in the Constitution in the sense of natural justice or the abstract.

Lex, not jus, was meant when the word "law" was employed. Therefore, the phrase "procedure established by law" would refer to the process outlined in an enacted statute. On the other side, Fazal Ali, J., disagreed with the majority's position and claimed that Article 21 should be amended to reflect the natural justice principle that "no one shall be condemned unheard."

According to how Article 21 was interpreted by the majority in the Gopalan case, it only placed restrictions on the executive branch, which could not act without a law, and it had no effect on the legislative branch, which could pass any law, no matter how draconian, restricting the rights of individuals without having to follow any reasonable procedures first. Whether or not the law provided for a fair or reasonable procedure was not for the court to decide.

The case of Maneka Gandhi v. Union of India demonstrates how liberal inclinations have shaped the supreme court's interpretation of fundamental rights, particularly Article 21. Following the tragic events of the emergency from 1975 to 1977, there has been a significant change in the judicial approach towards the protection of individual liberties.

The Maneka Gandhi case has had a significant impact on the evolution of Indian constitutional law. According to Bhagwati, J., Article 21 'embodies a constitutional value of Supreme importance in a democratic society'. Iyer, J., has characterized Article 21 as the procedural Magna Carta protective of life and liberty.

The Gopalan viewpoint, which had dominated the field for almost three decades, is entirely overthrown by Maneka case. Since Maneka, the Supreme Court has emphasised numerous times that Articles 14, 19, and 21 do not conflict with one another but rather support, reinforce, and nourish one another.

The Supreme Court has given a relatively liberal and broad interpretation to the term "life" in Article 21. The Court has increasingly given life a broad interpretation throughout time. The scope of the Article 21-guaranteed right to life includes both physical existence and quality of life. Any statutes that conflict with such a right must be declared unconstitutional.

In the Francis Coralie case, Bhagwati, J. stated: "We believe that the right to life includes the right to live with human dignity and all that goes along with it, namely, the basic necessities of life, such as adequate nutrition, clothing, and shelter over one's head, as well as facilities for reading, writing, and expressing oneself in various forms, freely moving about, and mixing and mingling with fellow human beings".

In Olga Tellis v. Bombay Municipal Corporation, the Supreme Court has decided that the term life in Article 21 is not only restricted to the mere animal existence of a person. It means something more and the inhibition against the deprivation of life extends to all those limits and faculties by which life is enjoyed.

<u>CONCLUSION</u>

Fundamental rights for citizens are upheld by a large number of countries around the world, particularly those with written constitutions. The ultimate law of the land protects these rights, which are more formalistic and technical in nature. For instance, the US Constitution guaranteed its citizens a variety of fundamental human rights through the Bill of Rights. Many nations around the world, especially those with written constitutions, uphold fundamental rights for citizens. These rights, which are primarily formalistic and technical in character, are safeguarded by the supreme law of the land. For instance, the US Constitution's Bill of Rights guaranteed its citizens a number of essential human rights. Thomas Jefferson said, "A Bill of Rights is what the people are entitled to against every government, and what no just government should refuse, or rest on inference." To ensure that they cannot be eliminated by customary legal processes, some fundamental and inherent human rights are specified and safeguarded under the constitution. Therefore, the idea of fundamental rights upholds human rights and makes sure that nobody is denied these essential rights. The protection of citizens' rights by a recognised authority is crucial because governments cannot be trusted. Therefore, a redressal mechanism is often included in most nations that guarantee fundamental rights, ensuring that these rights are fully enjoyed and not merely on paper.

The most significant right protected by our constitution is Article 21. It is the foundation upon which the entire structure of fundamental rights is built. The supreme court's progressive interpretation has continuously broadened this Article's scope and growth. It is a prime example which showcases the summation of human rights into one oscillating point. The interpretation of the Fundamental Right provided under Article 21 by the Judiciary made it evident that Fundamental Right do mirrors Human Right. And it is safe to expect that this flawless Article will continue to incorporate new elements.

Authors' Bio

Debarghya Bhattacharya is currently working as the Assistant Professor at Kristu Jayanti College of Law, Bengaluru and is pursuing M.Phil. in Law from Central University of Sikkim. He has completed his B.A.LL.B. (Honours) and LL.M. degrees from University of Calcutta. He stood first in the University of Calcutta in Master of Laws Examination, 2016 and received Order of Merit Certificate. His expertise includes Constitutional and Administrative Laws, Jurisprudence and Legal Methods, Human Rights Laws and Practice, Public International Law etc. He also has past experience in assisting Senior Counsel in Litigation at Alipore Judges Court, Kolkata. He has published articles in National and International Journals and blogs. He has also presented various papers at seminars and, attended several Faculty Development Programmes and Conferences.

Astha Sen is a student of BBA.LL.B. 1st year at Kristu Jayanti College of Law, Bengaluru. She has completed her Senior Secondary education from Vatsalya Senior Secondary School, Sagar. She has done internship at Speak-Up World Foundation, New Delhi; in area of social work, finance, marketing and environment, where she has also got the Best Performer of the Week Award as well. She has got Certificate of Participation for Kanooniyat's National PIL Drafting Competition, 2021. She has also attended seminars as part of her legal education.

CHAPTER THIRTEEN

FROM VICTIM TO VIXEN-SHE IS A FIGHTER

Author: Khushi Nayyar, III year of B.A.,LL.B. from University of Petroleum and Energy Studies, Dehardun

A woman is a full circle because she has the power to create, to nurture and to transform but why does the society disapprove of this fact? Gender Bias or discrimination has been a prevalent issue in our country for decades now. It refers to distribution of unequal rights between male and female based on different gender roles which further leads to unjust treatment. The differentiations in genders havealso led to unequal ratios of new born males and females in the country. On an average there are 105 males to every 100 females. As we look into the Crime Bureau Statistics record, we find that lots of atrocities are committed against women every day. The society has still not accepted women in public spaces and as a result, they face discrimination. Patriarchy breaches the value of Gender equality. The male supremacy has not led women to come up in areas which are predominantly occupied by men. The question that arises is- Aren't women trying to bring about a structural change in the community?

Women have never stopped trying to enhance their presence be it any field for that matter. In 1853, Savtribai Phule dedicated her life to championing the cause of the oppressed. It was Savitribai's crusade against Brahminical patriarchy that set the ball rolling for intersectional Feminism and education for all in our country. She with her husband established an education society that opened schools for girls and women. Tough situations and experiences make a person stronger and powerful. The famous Bollywood actor, Priyanka Chopra once shared that early on in her career when she was about eighteen or nineteen the director and producer told her that if she didn't agree to ridiculous terms or painfully low salary in his movie, he would just replace her because girls are replaceable in the entertainment business and that was the moment when she decided to become "IRREPLACEABLE".How can we contribute to growth when we can't achieve or create equal opportunities? Globally countries are losing over 160 trillion dollars of wealth because of the difference in earning between men and women. It is great that the Indian Government has created initiatives to promote skill development so that women can be a part of the workforce. Women empowerment is important because it is not an add-on to development; it is at the core of development for nations. Gender Gap to a large extent is closing since more women are being elected in government positions globally and economic empowerment is also happening as women are also earning.

Practices such as Female Infanticide, Dowry, Child Marriage and taboo on widow remarriage need to be rooted out especially in Northern India for women to lead a free and Independent life.The UN has adopted 7 principles to promote Gender Equality and Women Empowerment such as Treat all women and men fairly at work – respect and support human rights and nondiscrimination, Promote education, training and professional development for women, Implement enterprise development, supply chain and marketing practices that empower women, Ensure the health, safety and well-being of all women and men workers etc.

Gender equality is a basic human right, and it is also fundamental to having a peaceful, prosperous world. While some progress is being made in various parts of the world, there is still a great deal left to be done to right the problems of gender inequality.

Empowering women is essential to the health and social development of families, communities and countries. When women are living safe, fulfilled and productive lives, they can reach their full potential. A key part of this empowerment is through education. Girls who are educated can pursue meaningful work and contribute to their country's economy later in life. When women and girls are supported, they gain opportunities to speak up for their rights, and also to advocate for their communities. They are also able to rise in social standing, and they can feed this into future generations.The UN aims to eliminate all forms of violence against all women and girls in the public and private spheres, including trafficking and sexual and other types of exploitation, eliminate all harmful practices, such as child, early and forced marriage and female genital mutilation, recognize and value unpaid care and domestic work through the provision of public services, infrastructure and social protection policies and the promotion of shared responsibility within the household and the family as nationally appropriate, ensure women's full and effective participation and equal opportunities for leadership at all levels of decision making in political, economic and public life, enhance the use of enabling technology, in particular information and communications technology, to promote the empowerment of women, adopt and strengthen sound policies and enforceable legislation for the promotion of gender equality and the empowerment of all women and girls at all levels. Thus, Women's right is not only an abstraction, a cause; it is also a personal affair.

Author's Bio

Hello everyone. I'm khushi Nayyar and this is my first blog publication. My hometown belongs to Jamshedpur, Jharkhand. I've done my schooling from Scindia Kanya Vidyalaya, Gwalior and for my further studies I'm pursuing law from university of petroleum and energy studies, Dehradun. This is my 3rd year at college and I'm pretty excited to explore the new opportunities and grab the new learning that comes my way. I'm grateful to Brillopedia and Lawctopus for proving me this wonderful opportunity.

SOLOGAMY A FAD OR AN INSTITUTION

Author: Maria Tessa Sibin, I year of B.B.A.,LL.B. from Kristu Jayanti College of Law

Co-author: Anagha Joshy, I year of B.B.A.,LL.B. from Kristu Jayanti College of Law

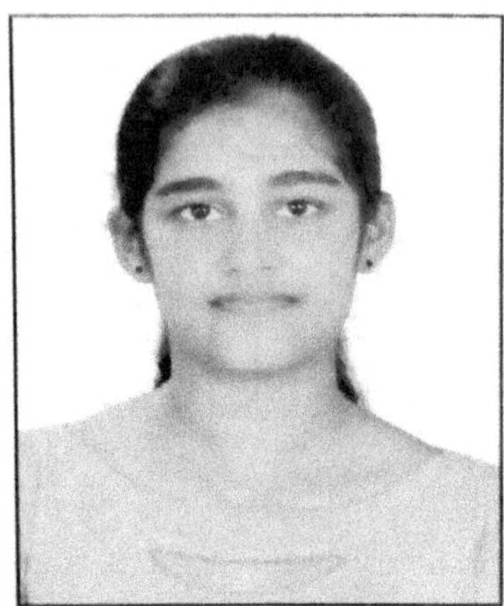

Co-author: Benlin Joseph, I year of B.B.A.,LL.B. from Kristu Jayanti College of Law

The world around us is changing in a fast-paced manner. Due to the busy schedules of us people, we tend to focus on these changes around us.

But one topic which caught our attention was the news of sologamy which happened in our country. The word Sologamy was not popular in our Indian society until Kshama Bindu from Gujarat decided to marry herself. It arose as a sensational issue as it was the first sologamy in our country. Sologamy or Autogamy or Self marriage refers to marriage by a person to themselves and affirms one's own value and leads to a happier life. There is Greek mythology about Narcissus a charming young man who won the hearts of all the lovely women. However, Narcissus chose to focus on being attractive himself over their devotion. He stooped to sip from a crystal-clear source of water while strolling through the woodland one day. He immediately fell in love with himself since he was so mesmerized by his own reflection in the pool. He lost his life while swimming for his own reflection in the water. This is believed to be the beginning of the practice of sologamy. According to our culture, marriage is a sacred relationship between two people (a man and a woman) that unites different families, cultures etc.based on mutual understanding. A relationship is united by god. Through sologamy Kshama Bindu has given a different dimension to the concept of marriage. Sologamy may look like a new concept but this was a known practice in Europe and other countries. Linda Baker US resident in the year 1993 married herself which turned out to be the first socialized sologamy marriage. In a country like India where the idea of same-sex marriage is not still accepted by society, the practice of sologamy is drastic. Everyone will have different concepts about their marriage, life partner etc. Through sologamy, Kshama Bindu revealed about her self-love.ie, love towards oneself. She said that she never wanted to get married. However, wanted to become a bride, so she decided to marry herself. Later she understood that she is the first example of self-love in our country. Self-marriage is a commitment to be there for oneself. It is an act of self-acceptance. People marry someone they love, she loved herself, and so she married herself. Through this marriage, she tried to portray that women matters. This was the concept of Kshama Bindu on sologamy. But several people opposed her wedding as it was against the traditions, cultures and religious beliefs of our country and did not allow her to marry inside the temple.

On 6 September 2018, the Supreme Court issued its verdict. The Court unanimously ruled that Section 377 is unconstitutional as it infringed on the fundamental rights of autonomy, intimacy, and identity, thus legalizing homosexuality in India. So one question arises, if homosexuality is legalized, then the concept sologamy or self-love can also be accepted.

We should also move according to the changing scenarios of society and concepts. Sologamy is the proclamation of self-acceptance, liberalization and understanding of oneself. It purely means loving oneself from the bottom of the heart. In simple words, we can say that taking vows to oneself. Let's look at different dimensions of thoughts on why people want to get married to themselves. Sologamy is the proclamation of self-acceptance, liberalization and understanding of oneself. In simple words, we can say that taking vows to oneself. Let's look at different dimensions of thoughts why people want to get married to themselves. In another point of view, suppose if a person is born physicallyhandicapped or with small disabilities, sometimes the society denies them good marriage proposals. From their point of view, they are also humans, like all others they will also have the desire to dress up like a bride or a groom and perform all rituals of marriage The good part of self-love or sologamy is that if it allows a person to be in contact with oneself, to love oneself, to admire oneself, to love all the inabilities of oneself, etc.

Society thinks that if this practice of sologamy is practiced the family lineage will be concerned. From the point of view of society, it is correct because for a country to grow it needs it citizens and if they practice it might effect the growth of the country. The practice of sologamy is not legalized in the country senior lawyer Chandrakant Gupta said, "The Hindu Marriage Act uses the terminology 'either of the spouse', which simply means that there must be two persons to complete the marriage. Sologamy will never pass the legal scrutiny." Sologamy can be related to Narcissistic personality disorder where a person has an inflated sense of their own importance, excessive admiration, or self-love. It is said that there are three elements involved in giving importance to self, lack of fruitful relationship,and using various strategies to give importance to herself/himself. It is a belief that the person thinks he is smarter or more attractivethan others this makes them fall into egocentric and they think society is against them. Instead, they want to see themselves as supreme and competent. They are less concerned with social warmth and social intimacy and they exhibit disinterest insharing and caring in romantic relationships. Sologamy has similar traits to NPD and many of the factors involved in NPD can be related to Sologamy like the admiration for self-love etc. Sologamy is tearing down the institution of marriage. Even though the concept of marriage has been diversified in many religions it is been challenged from many angles. Such practices include same-sex marriage, polygamy, and now SOLOGAMY.

people who are independent and have no need for emotional support from others may choose to do so. "If we look deeper, attachment styles like avoidant/rejective styles can account for people not believing they need someone to make them feel whole. They are independent and feel "enough" for themselves. Secure attachment type people are those in a healthy relationship with themselves. They are not afraid of being alone and don't believe that being alone equals loneliness. They are emotionally very strong beings," says the relationship expert. one who runs the risk of becoming so independent that the need for social interaction can be greatly reduced. The psychologist say's it can get lonely for some – not in a bad, hopeless way – but in a way where you can start showing narcissistic tendencies.A single man may not be a good citizen. He may become hard-hearted as he has never had a companion throughout his life. Many religions consider marriage as a sacred enactment and such acts are hampering such practices. Marriage has traditionally been viewed in the Christian tradition as a lifelong, conjugal covenant between a man and a woman, a union of love that entails dedicating oneself to God and to others. Other religions have their own viewpoint of marriage but all point toward the same direction in which marriage is a sacred practice.

It's the situations that make people change their decision which they have already taken. This has happened in the case of Sologamy. Brazilian model and social media influencer Cris Galêra has ended her sologamy marriage just 90 days after she found out someone more special. She stated that this act gave her pleasure only for a short period of time but she said that she found love and she decided to end this practice. This is evident that the human mind or decision taken by a person can shift We can say that it might be just for a short time or we can say that the particular person considers that they require only themselves and there is no one they need for support. It' 's just something which is done for media publicity and nothing more and it's like they are trying to prove that they are correct and that society is wrong which is absolutely wrong. Sologamy has received a lot of criticism for being narcissistic and self-indulgent. While there might be merit in that, there seems to be something even more disturbing going on here. It is downright pathetic and is the exact opposite of empowerment for sologamists, however, there seems to be a need to commemorate this very basic commitment to oneself in the most patriarchal ceremony. Yes, marriage is founded on patriarchy. Anybody who has looked into the history of how matrimony came about will know that it was more about economics and child-rearing than love. So, the need to solemnizeself-love in a ritual that is rooted in something that is, in fact, antithetical to empowerment is stupid. sologamists are not opposed to the idea of dating someone else.

Sophie Tanner, a sologamist hailing from Brighton, told a popular publication, 'People think if you marry yourself you gain a nun status, but obviously, if you're a nun you commit your body to God. This is committing yourself to yourself. You can still love everyone else. It's the decision of every individual and it's their choice how to live this life.It depends from person to person, their attitude, their social surroundings etc. So never criticize anyone for their uniqueness. That uniqueness makes them different from others. Let them be unique in their own ways and just allow them to create their own history. But do you support a practice like this?

<u>Authors' Bio</u>

Maria Tessa Sibin is a student of BBA.LL.B. 1st year at Kristu Jayanti College of Law, Bengaluru. She has completed her Senior Secondary education atSacred Heart Higher Secondary School, Thiruvambady. She has done an internship at Umeed - A drop of hope, New Delhi; in the area of social work, finance, and marketing an environment, where she has also got the Best Performer of the Week Award as well. She has got a Certificate of Presentationfor XII National Online Conference on Emerging Trends in Rule of Law, Democratic Norms, and Constitutional Values organized by National Conference Committee, 2021-22, School of Law, CHRIST (Deemed to be University).Awarded with Rajyapuraskar in Bharat Scout and Guides.Participated in State-level National Children's Science Congress (NCSC). She has also attended seminars as part of her legal education.

Anagha Joshy is a student of BBA.LL.B. 1st year at Kristu Jayanti College of Law, Bengaluru. She has completed her Senior Secondary education atSt. Thomas Higher Secondary School, Thomapuram. She has done an internship at Umeed - A drop of hope, New Delhi; in the area of social work, finance, and marketing an environment. She has got a Certificate of Presentationfor XII National Online Conference on Emerging Trends in Rule of Law, Democratic Norms, and Constitutional Values organized by National Conference Committee, 2021-22, School of Law, CHRIST (Deemed to be University).Secured 3rd prize in district-level badminton.Certificate of Appreciation DLI Student Ambassador Program conducted By LSAC Global. Webinar onAwareness Program on IP and Entertainment organized by DPIIT-IR Maharashtra National Law University. She has also attended seminars as part of her legal education.

Benlin Joseph is a student of BCOM.LL.B. 1st year at Kristu Jayanti College of Law, Bengaluru. He has completed his Senior Secondary education from Birla Public School, Qatar He has done an internship at Umeed - A drop of hope New Delhi; in the area of social work, finance, and marketing environment, where she has also got the Best Performer of the Week Award as well. He has got a Certificate of Presentationfor XII National Online Conference on Emerging Trends in Rule of Law, Democratic Norms, and Constitutional Values organized by National Conference Committee, 2021-22, School of Law, CHRIST (Deemed to be University).Has Completed Grade 4 from Trinity College London for Piano, Keyboard. Has Completed a Toastmaster training program in 2017. He has also attended seminars as part of her legal education